Ask

for the

Old Paths

A call for God's people
to return to God's word

John Hobbs

Heritage Publications
1106 Destiny Court
Wylie, Texas 75098

Contents

Chapter	Title	Page
	Introduction	v
1	Must the Church of Christ Change to Grow?	9
2	Examining Ourselves	25
3	Returning to God?	39
4	Restoring the New Testament Church	53
5	The New Testament Pattern	67
6	Acceptable Worship to God	77
7	Instrumental Music in Worship? #1	89
8	Instrumental Music in Worship? #2	103
9	The New Testament Teaching on Baptism #1	117
10	The New Testament Teaching on Baptism #2	131
11	The Churches of Christ Were Right after All	143
12	Is the Church of Christ a Cult?	155
	About the Author	169

Introduction

When Judah was living in sin, God because of his "great love" (Jer. 31:3; Isa. 63:9; Eph. 2: 5) pleaded with Judah to return to Him. In Jeremiah 6:16 we read, "Thus saith Jehovah, Stand ye in the ways and see, and **ask for the old paths, where is the good way; and walk therein**, and ye shall find rest for your souls: but they said, We will not walk therein." The cure for their problem was "ask for the old paths, where is the good way; and walk therein." But, they refused. How sad! How tragic! Moses many years before Jeremiah said, "Oh that they were wise, that they understood this, that they would consider their latter end!" (Deut. 32:29). Judah should have considered their latter end! The preaching of Jeremiah was around 627 B.C. Jeremiah warned them of the impending disaster. But, they refused to repent and hearken to Jeremiah. God said, "No man repenteth him of his wickedness, saying, What have I done?" (Jer. 8:6). Again God said, "Behold, I will enter into judgment with thee, because thou sayest, I have not sinned" (Jer. 2:35). In 586 B. C. the nation of Judah was destroyed by the Babylonians. Many died by the sword and famine. The slaughter was horrible. But, Judah brought the destruction on themselves because they refused to walk in the old paths. The Churches of Christ need to learn from this history lesson.

Before Moses died, he told the Israelites, "Remember the days of old. Consider the years of many generations: Ask thy father, and he will show thee; thine elders, and they will tell thee" (Deut. 32:7). In other words listen to those who are older than you. Oh how I wish brethren in the Church of Christ would do that today! I have changed my mind on several theological positions because I listened to older preachers. I am not saying that just because a preacher is older that makes him right. But, at least listen to them.

Today in the Churches of Christ we have brethren who seem to think that if we will loosen our theology, allow women to participate in the worship service, allow women to be elders and preachers, use the piano and solos and choirs and praise teams, take down the sign "Church of Christ" in front of the building, and stop insisting that baptism is necessary for salvation, that suddenly people will flock to our services. Some say we need to have services that are invigorating and praise teams help to do just that. But, the main question is what does God want—not what we want. The apostle Paul warned, "For the time will come when they will not endure the sound doctrine; but, having itching ears, will heap to themselves teachers after their own lusts; and will turn away their ears from the truth, and turn aside unto fables" (2 Tim. 4:3-4).

This book is designed for Churches of Christ to **"ask for the old paths, where is the good way, and walk therein."** We have too many "change-agents" in our brotherhood that want to change our worship and theology. I want to take a serious re-examination of key concepts like worship, instrumental music, and baptism. My goal is to go back to the Bible and let God's word be the final determining factor in all religious matters. We absolutely refuse to be led by "human tradition." Worship needs to be directed by God's word—not by that which is invigorating.

"Change" is in the air. The question we must ask is: "Change from what to what?" Why should we change from what has worked? (From 1945 to 1965 the Churches of Christ were the fastest growing religious body in America. Why do we want to change what worked?") Why should we change to that which God will not accept? Wisdom says we reject changes that depart from God's will. We have too many brethren who are being led by their own understanding. God says, "Lean not upon thine own understanding" (Prov. 3:5). My prayer is that we will **"ask for the old paths, where is the good way; and walk therein."**

1

Must The Church of Christ Change To Grow?

This is a very important, relevant, and timely topic! We have some preachers, elders, professors, and editors in our brotherhood who are saying that we must change to grow. They also claim that if we do not change, we will die. At the ACU 2001 Bible Lectureship, Randy Harris, a Bible professor at ACU said, "We're in trouble in Churches of Christ . . . We're not making any converts. We are dead in the water." While it is true that many Churches of Christ are not growing—some are!

Some people seem to think that if we will loosen our theology, allow women to participate in the public worship service, allow women to be elders and preach, use the piano and solos and choirs and praise teams in our services, take down the sign "Church of Christ" in front of the building, and stop insisting that baptism is necessary for salvation, that suddenly people will flock to our services. We need a thorough examination of this concept. The most important question to ask is: Even if these things would work, would God approve of doing them?

Lessons from History

In north Israel Jeroboam changed the place of worship (from Jerusalem to Dan and Bethel), the object of worship (from Jehovah God to two golden calves), the priesthood (from Levites to the lowest of the people; 1 Kings 12:31), and the feast day from the 15th day 7th month to the 15th day 8th month; Lev. 23:34). These were all clear violations of God's word. How does the word of God view all these changes? 1 Kings 12:30 emphatically states, "And this thing became a sin."

Jeroboam's worship was one in which "he devised of his own heart" (1 Kings 12:33). His plan of worship did not come from God; it came from his own mind. In order for our worship to be accepted by God, we must worship with the right purpose of heart and the external act must conform to God's word (John 4:24). The apostle Paul condemned "will-worship" in Colossians 2:23. "Will-worship" is when man worships the way he wills –instead of the way God wills. Therefore, it is not accepted by God!

God through Isaiah said to the Israelites long ago, "Woe to the rebellious children, saith Jehovah, that take counsel, but not of me" (Isa. 30:1). The people said to the prophets, "Prophesy not unto us right things, speak unto us smooth things, prophesy deceits" (Isa. 30:10). God called their actions "iniquity" (Isa. 30:13). Notice their attitude. They did not want the truth. They wanted a feel-good religion, one that allowed them to do what they wanted. Because they refused to hearken to the word of God, "There came **great wrath** from Jehovah of

hosts" (Zech. 7:12). Not just wrath but **"great wrath."**
Departure from the word of God always brings His
severe chastisement and punishment!

Jeremiah 5:30-31 states, "A wonderful (i.e. an
astonishing and amazing thing) and horrible thing is
come to pass in the land: the prophets prophesy falsely,
and the priests bear rule by their means (notice not God's
means); and my people love to have it so: and what will
ye do in the end thereof?" What Jeremiah said about
Judah applies today to God's people. It is sad but true
that some of our brethren "love to have it so." Some
brethren want change and they do not care what God's
word says. Sad!

Jeremiah 6:16 states, **"Thus saith Jehovah, Stand
ye in the ways and see, and ask for the old paths,
where is the good way; and walk therein, and ye shall
find rest for your souls: but they said, We will not
walk therein."** Notice the "old paths" is the "good
way." God loved Judah (Jer. 31:3) and wanted them to
return to Him and obey Him so they could be blessed.
But they said, "We will not walk therein." Our brethren
need to ask for the old paths, i.e. God's paths, the good
way, the way of righteousness. John wrote, "He that
doeth righteousness is righteous" (1 John 3:7).

Paul wrote, "For whatsoever things were written
aforetime were written for our learning, that through
patience and through comfort of the scriptures we might
have hope" (Rom. 15:4). If we are wise, we will learn
from these history lessons. It is always sin to change
what God has legislated and required. It is extremely
important to realize that when God has instructed us on

"how to worship" Him in a certain way, that rules out what we want or what we feel or what we think!

The Nature of Truth

The definition of truth is "conformity with fact; an established or verified fact; corresponding to reality; correctness; accuracy." Since facts do not change, truth does not change. I was born on a certain day. That is truth that will never change. $2 + 2 = 4$. This is a mathematical truth that will never change. When I go to bed and get up the next morning, $2 + 2$ is still equal to 4. This is one reason I like teaching math.

Several years ago I was teaching a math class. One girl raised her hand and said, "I am 12 today and in 2 years I will be 14. So, truth changes." I told her, "You are 12 today. That is truth. In 2 years, you will be 14. That is truth. There is no contradiction between these truths. The truth is not changing—your age is changing. Truth never changes!" The speed limit used to be 70 mph. Then it was 55, then 65, and now it is 70. Did the truth change? No! The speed limit changed. When I got married, I weighed 230 pounds. Now I weigh 230 plus none of your business. Did the truth change? No! My weight changed.

In 1975, I took my first course on my first Master's degree. The professor had a Doctor's degree. One day after class the professor said, "John I want to see you in my office for a few minutes." I had turned in a short paper where I had used the word "always" several times. He had circled the word in pencil every time I had used it. He told me that things are not always the same so I needed to be very careful with using the word always. I said that if something is true, it is always true because truth does not change. He said I was wrong because truth sometimes does change. I asked him would he please give me an example where truth changes. Here is his response, "Before Columbus discovered America, everyone thought the world was flat. Then after he discovered America, people realized the world was round and not flat. Therefore, the truth changed." I very quickly said, "Wait just a minute. Before Columbus discovered America, the world was round. It has always been round. The truth did not change—only man's conception of the truth changed." He leaned back in his chair and looked at me with complete amazement. After thinking for a few seconds he said, "You know I think you are right."

Some have told me, "John don't you know the new math teaches $2 + 2 = 10$. Therefore, the truth changes." Yes, $2 + 2 = 10$ in base four. But, in base ten $2 + 2 = 4$. These are two different mathematical truths that do not contradict and will never change!

Spiritually, the word of God is truth. Jesus said, "Sanctify them in the truth: thy word is truth" (John 17:17). David said, "Thy words are truth" (2 Sam. 7:28). The psalmist wrote, "Thy law is truth" (Psa. 119:142) and "All thy commandments are truth" (Psa. 119:151). The apostle Paul talked about "the word of truth" (2 Tim. 2:15). Paul wrote to the church at Thessalonica and said they received the message "as it is in truth, the word of God" (2 Thess. 2:13). **Spiritual truth is the word of God that does not change!** By the very definition of truth, the Bible contains eternal and unchanging truth.

Many people today are looking for something that is true and permanent. They want something that can be trusted and will not change. They want something they can depend on and will be a guide for their lives. Sadly, unfortunately, they do not realize that the Bible contains the eternal truth that can give them direction they need to enter into heaven. 2 Timothy 3:16-17 KJV states, "All Scripture is given by the inspiration of God and is profitable for doctrine, for reproof, for correction, for instruction in righteousness, that the man of God may be perfect, thoroughly furnished unto all good works." Paul said in Acts 20:32, "And now I commend you to God, and to the word of his grace, which is able to build you up, and give you the inheritance among all them that are sanctified."

The Role of the Church

Paul wrote, "These things write I unto thee, hoping to come unto thee shortly; but If I tarry long, that thou mayest know how men ought to behave themselves in the house of God, which is the church of the living God, the pillar and ground of the truth" (1 Tim. 3:14-15). Thus, the role of the Church is to be the pillar and ground of the truth. In other words we are to preach and teach the truth without apology! According to 2 Timothy 4:2, we are to "reprove" and "rebuke" those who teach false doctrine. Yes, we will do it in love (Eph. 4:15). Love "rejoiceth with the truth" (1 Cor. 13:4). Love does not rejoice with error and false doctrine.

Paul warned, "For the time will come when they will not endure the sound doctrine; but, having itching ears, will heap to themselves teachers after their own lusts; and will turn away their ears from the truth, and turn aside unto fables" (2 Tim. 4:3-4). Notice that some Christians "will turn away their ears from the truth." We are witnessing the fulfillment of the inspired Word in our lifetime.

Again, Paul wrote, "So then, brethren, stand fast, and hold the traditions which ye were taught, whether by word, or by epistle of ours" (2 Thess. 2:15). The word "epistle" refers to the written word of God. W.E. Vine defines the word "traditions" as "a handing down or on." Vine points out that there are traditions of men and traditions of God. The traditions of men are not from God and not authoritative (Matt. 15:1-9; Mark 7:1-9). There are "traditions" of God which are binding and authoritative (cf. 1 Cor. 11:2; 2 Thess. 2:15—Vine says by metonymy in these verses "traditions" means "apostolic teaching"). **Please note that the inspired apostle taught "hold the teachings!" He did not say to change them!** The church's responsibility is to teach and preach the apostolic teachings. We are not to go beyond the written word (1 Cor. 4:6). What Paul wrote are the commandments of the Lord (1 Cor. 14:37). On the Day of Judgment, we will be "judged out of the things that are written in the books" (Rev. 20:12). The "books" are the books of the Bible (John 12:48; Acts 17:30-31; Psa. 119:172).

Brethren who hold a loose view of the authority of Scripture are making an eternal mistake. Jesus said, "Man shall not live by bread alone but by every word that proceedeth out of the mouth of God" (Matt. 4:4). Every time Jesus was tempted to sin, He said, "It is written." He had the highest regard for the written word of God.

He said, "For verily I say unto you, Till heaven and earth pass away, one jot or one tittle shall in no wise pass away from the law, till all things be accomplished" (Matt. 5:18). The "jot" was the smallest Hebrew letter and the "tittle" was a very tiny part of a Hebrew letter. By referring to the letters of the written word of God, Jesus believed in the authority of the written word of God. We must do likewise (1 John 2:6; 1 Pet. 2:21).

Methods Can Change But Not the Message

Jesus said, "Go ye into all the world, and preach the gospel to the whole creation" (Mark 16:15). Jesus told us to "go" and "preach." He did not tell us how. The how is left up to us. No one can bind the how. God has left that up to us.

Several years ago in Arkansas, a man got up to preach with an overhead projector. Many people labeled him a false teacher because he used this method. They said, "Jesus just taught. Paul just taught. So it is wrong to use an overhead projector." But brethren, Jesus taught us to be "wise as serpents, and harmless as doves" (Matt. 10:16). Jesus never used a PA system, radio, TV, computer, etc. Does this mean it is wrong for us to use these things? No! Methods of teaching the gospel can change but we must never change the message.

One Sunday morning in Alabama many years ago, the preacher told the song leader not to lead a song after the prayer because he had a longer sermon than usual. (Normally they had 3 songs, a prayer, a song, and then the sermon.) After the prayer, the preacher got up into the pulpit to preach. An elder stood up and said, "Song leader get up there and lead one more song. We are going to make this worship service scriptural." We must understand that human tradition is not binding. The order of a worship service is not written in stone.

One time a little girl asked her mother why she cut off the ends of the ham before she cooked it. The mother replied, "I don't know. My mother always did." Her daughter pressed her for a good reason. They called the grandmother and asked her why she cut off the ends of the ham before she cooked it. The grandmother replied, "I do not know. My mother always did." So, they called the great-grandmother. She told them the reason she cut off the ends of the ham before she cooked it was because her pan was not big enough. What started off with a good reason soon became a "human tradition."

In every generation the Church of Christ will always need to go back and analyze Scripture. The Church must determine what is binding and authoritative compared with what is "human tradition" which is not binding. This demands that we must be good students of the word of God. This is an absolute must! Human tradition and methods can change. But, the truth of the word of God must be seen as the unchanging eternal truth to guide our lives. We must absolutely never compromise the truth of Scripture!

The Religious World Today

Time magazine, April 5, 1991, said, "Today a quiet revolution is taking place that is changing not only the religious habits of millions of Americans, but the way churches go about recruiting members to keep their doors open. Increasing numbers of baby boomers who left the fold years ago are turning religious again, but many are traveling from church to church or faith to faith, sampling creeds, shopping for a custom-made god." Brethren, this is absolute foolishness. We cannot make God into the kind of God we want. We cannot make Christianity into a kind of religion that we want. Proverbs 14:12 states, "There is a way which seemeth right unto a man; But the end thereof are the ways of death."

Today, throughout the religious world, people are leaving churches in droves. From 1965 to 2005 the following denominations have lost members:

Lutherans	12%
Methodists	29%
Episcopalians	35%
Presbyterians	47%
Disciples of Christ	60%

In 2010, figures from a study revealed that the mainline Protestant churches have continued the decline. Where do we (Churches of Christ) stand? First of all, since we are by Scripture locally autonomous (1 Pet. 5:2; Acts 20:28), we do not have good records. Dr. Mac Lynns' book reveals we are also losing members. Some Churches of Christ have decided to cut their ties with our fellowship which has caused a significant decline in numbers.

Change Agents in the Brotherhood

On Tuesday, October 5, 1999, Michael Light, a faithful gospel preacher, went to Highland Church of Christ in Abilene, Texas. Michael observed Eddie Sharp, who was the pulpit minister of the University Church of Christ in Abilene and ACU Bible professor, serve the Lord's Supper to the "Walk to Emmaeus" group there that night. There was also a live band in the building. By what authority can we partake of the Lord's Supper on Tuesday night or use musical instruments? The New Testament plainly teaches we are to observe the Lord's Supper on the first day of the week (Acts 20:7). In 1 Cor. 11:26, Paul instructs the Christians, "For as often as ye eat this bread and drink the cup, ye proclaim the Lord's death till he come." The question is how "often" is "often"? That is answered in 1 Cor. 16:2—"upon the first day of every week." The church came together on the "the first day of every week" to partake of the Lord's Supper and give as they had been prospered. Church history is clear that the early Christians observed the Lord's Supper on the first day of every week. Whatever we do in religious matters, we must have authority (Col. 3:17). There is no authority for Tuesday night! Sharp was guilty of "will-worship" (Col. 2:23). An elder of the University Church of Christ told me that there has never been a public confession of sin from Sharp. Why? Because he does not believe he sinned. Recognition of sin is the first step in the repentance process (Jer. 2:35; 8:4-6). Michael Light wrote, "Sharp plainly and specifically taught that it does not matter where you worship or what tradition of faith you're in, just serve Jesus. Sharp said we are to follow the light of Jesus wherever it leads us. If it leads you to stay in your current church fine, if it leads us to change churches then we should do just that." Brethren—there is only "one body" (Eph. 4:4; 1 Cor. 12:12, 13, 20; Rom. 12:4-5; Col. 3:15)! Since the "body" is the "church" and the "church" is the "body"—Eph. 1:22-23; Col. 1:18, there is only one church. Jesus only promised to build one church, he only died for one church, he is only going to save one church (Matt. 16:16-18; Eph. 5:22-25; Acts 2:47). Division is sinful (Gal. 5:19-21; 1 Cor. 1:10-13). Staying in a religious body that is not the Lord's will not bring salvation. The only solution is go back to the Bible as the full and final and authoritative guide in everything we do (Acts 20:32).

In a Bible class on preaching at ACU several years ago, Andre Resner was the teacher. He used ten preachers he considered as examples of "great preachers." Resner used Dr. Thomas Long as an example of a "great preacher." Chuck Pearson was a student in the class. Chuck said, "Dr. Long is a Presbyterian minister. He is not a Christian." (Note: Long was Resner's mentor while he pursued a doctorate at Princeton). Resner responded that Chuck could not know that and that only God knew who was or was not a Christian. Chuck answered back that he had been a Presbyterian before he became a Christian and could confidently say that the Princeton professor had not obeyed the gospel and was therefore not a Christian! (cf. Rom. 6:3-4, 17-18; Acts 2:38, 22:16; Mark 16:16; 1 Pet. 3:21; 1 Cor. 12:13; etc.) Chuck rebuked Resner (2 Tim. 4:2) by saying it was inappropriate for using this material for teaching students to be gospel preachers since all ten preachers were members of denominations. Thus, they did not teach the truth on how to become a Christian or how to worship "in "spirit and truth." They did not preach the gospel plan of salvation. Resner interrupted Chuck and raised his voice and said, "I know where you are going with this, and we're not going to go there in this class." Amazing—Resner did not want to discuss "how" a person becomes a Christian. And just think— Resner taught in one of our Universities. Titus 1:10-11 says that the mouths of false teachers "must be stopped." Unfortunately, sadly, the wrong mouth got stopped that day.

One ACU professor, in his church bulletin, wrote about William Carey, the great "Baptist" preacher. He wrote that Carey "was discouraged by Christian leaders" from being a missionary. But brethren--Carey's leaders were "Baptist leaders" who taught "Baptist doctrine" and "Baptist baptism." They did not teach that baptism is "unto the remission of sins." Baptists distort and twist and pervert the purpose of baptism. Therefore, their kind of baptism is not "in spirit and truth."

On page 124 in the book *The Crux of the Matter* published by ACU Press, Jeff Childers, Douglas Foster, and Jack Reese state that we have been "extremely sectarian by effectively denying that anyone outside our churches could be a true Christian." By their reliance on the "Lunenburg Letters" by Alexander Campbell, they would even include the un-immersed as Christians. In other words they are saying that the kind of baptism one has experienced does not make any difference. To them the mode—immersion, sprinkling, or pouring, or rose petals etc. is indifferent. They also consider the purpose to be indifferent. Is baptism "unto the remission of sins" (*eis aphesin ton hamartion*) or is it "because of remission of sins" (*dia aphesin ton hamartion*)? What makes them think they have the right to change what God Almighty has said through His word? They do not have the right! We do not have the right! No one does! They are committing a "presumptuous sin" (Psa. 19:13). Nadab and Abihu were destroyed because they offered "strange fire"—i.e. unlawful fire unto the Lord (Lev. 10:1-2). "Our God is a consuming fire" (Heb. 12:29). "It is a fearful thing to fall into the hands of the living God" (Heb. 10:31). The apostle Paul said there is "one faith, one baptism" (Eph. 4:5). This one baptism is by immersion. This is exactly what the Greek word *baptizo* means! It is also "unto the remission of sins" (Acts 2:38; Matt. 26:28). Therefore, anyone who has not been immersed for the right reason has not experienced the "one baptism" of Eph. 4:5 and is not a Christian. Period! This is Christian truth. If we are going to speak the "oracles of God" (1 Pet. 4:11), we must teach this. This may not be popular but it is Bible truth. Saying the "sinner's prayer" and asking Jesus to come into your heart does not make one a Christian.

Brethren, today we have change-agents in our brotherhood who want to change the name, the worship, and the doctrine of the Lord's Church. They want to de-hydrate the Bible and refrigerate hell. They want to bring in a piano, praise teams, choirs, and solos. They want to accept denominational baptism and have the Lord's Supper any time. One ignorant Christian said, "It's a shame we could not have had the Lord's Supper yesterday (i.e. Saturday) at the picnic, and the only reason we couldn't is because of CHURCH OF CHRIST tradition." These change-agents want to re-define the role of women in the Church and allow women to preach and teach. (One elder said he would have no problem with women serving as elders.) Some even want to teach the continuance of miraculous gifts. We have ignorant elders and preachers who are leading Christians away from the truth. Dr. J. C. Davis, a New Testament Greek scholar in our brotherhood, said ignorant elders "are as dangerous as sectarian ministers." He is right!

Conclusion

Faithful brethren will not sit idly by and say nothing. Righteous Christians will oppose this ungodliness. Paul said, "So then am I become your enemy, by telling you the truth?" (Gal. 4:16). Faithful brethren should expect opposition. Jesus said, "Woe unto you, when all speak well of you! For in the same manner did their fathers to the false prophets" (Luke 6:26). The liberal brethren who read this book will not like me or agree with me. But, I am not preaching to please them. I am preaching to please God Almighty. Paul wrote, "For am I now seeking the favor of men, or of God? Or am I striving to please men? If I were still pleasing men, I should not be a servant of Christ" (Gal. 1:10). Paul said, "Hold the teachings"—he did not say change them!

For Thought or Discussion

1. How did Jeroboam lead north Israel into sin?
2. What was the attitude of the Israelites in Jer. 5:30-31?
3. What was God's response to the unfaithful in Jer. 6:16?
4. Discuss the nature of truth.
5. What is the authoritative guide for Christians today? Scriptures?
6. What is the role of the Church today?
7. How did Jesus view the written word of God? Scripture?
8. Is "human tradition" binding today?
9. What is the job of every generation of Christians?
10. What kind of religion should we seek?
11. Discuss the change-agents we have in the brotherhood.
12. What did Jesus teach in Luke 6:26?
13. What does the Greek word *baptizo* mean?
14. What is the purpose of baptism from Acts 2:38?
15. What does Hebrews 10:31 and 12:29 say about God?
16. What is the force of Paul's statement "Hold the teachings" in 2 Thessalonians 2:15?

2

Examining Ourselves

The apostle Paul said, "Examine yourselves" **(KJV--2 Cor. 13:5).** I strongly believe that we need to take a long, hard, and serious look at ourselves. Any business or organization or sports team will examine itself and seek for improvement. Churches of Christ need to do the same thing! Gary Hill, an elder and concerned Christian, wrote, "I am afraid that too many times we are rushing after a failed denominational growth model that if only we would pause and observe the obvious it might alter out flight to 'change.' The many 'change agents' in our midst are rushing into growth models and practices that are not going to produce the results we so desire." Gary is right on target! Gary also wrote, "I think it is healthy to pause once in a while and take inventory of where we are . . . in our personal journey of faith, our local congregation and yes our entire fellowship. I must say that when I pause to reflect on what is going on in our fellowship I am not encouraged! I am afraid that we are slowly but surely losing our way!" Sadly, I agree with Gary. I wonder what Jeremiah would have said if he observed the departures that were going on in the brotherhood these days? Let us honestly examine where we are and where we are going.

How Does the Holy Spirit Work in Growth?

Randy Harris said that growth would come about not by "human wisdom" but by "the work of God's Holy Spirit." His statement is Calvinistic. He needs to read carefully 1 Corinthians 3:6 where Paul said, "I planted, Apollos watered, but God gave the increase." Growth is not so mysterious as many believe. To take the importance of our efforts out of the salvation equation is to deny the plain teaching of Scripture. Notice how the Parable of the Sower starts off, "The sower went forth to sow his seed" (Luke 8:4). Notice the human effort in the parable and the necessity of humans in planting the seed! Luke 8:11 states, "The seed is the word of God." Yes, we need to pray for God's guidance to help us. Yes, we need to pray for the Lord to help us to decide in what person, town, city, or nation to preach the seed of the kingdom. But, the Holy Spirit is going to work through the word of God to bring about growth. The Book of Acts clearly teaches that salvation comes about by people hearing the word of God. In the ten cases of conversion in Acts, not one was by a direct operation of the Holy Spirit. A miracle brought some preachers to the lost but the actual conversion process was by the simple planting and sowing the seed of the kingdom. **It must be forcefully and emphatically said that the seed does not plant itself! We are the ones who sow the seed of the kingdom (Luke 8:4; 1 Cor. 3:6).** The Holy Spirit is not going to work on the heart of a lost person in a "direct" way! The Holy Spirit is not going to plant the seed of the kingdom. The direct operation of the Holy Spirit is Calvinism pure and simple and thus false doctrine.

There is a fable that goes like this. After Jesus ascended into heaven, Michael, the archangel, asked Jesus, "What plans have you made for the salvation of men?" Jesus responded, "I have entrusted the gospel message with twelve men who are to take the gospel to the whole world. They are also to teach others to preach the gospel who will teach others to preach the gospel" (Mark 16:15-16; 2 Tim. 2:2). Michael said, "What if they do not do this?" Jesus said, "I have no other plan." If people are going to hear the gospel, they will hear it because we plant the seed of the kingdom into their hearts. This is not the work of human wisdom, but the "obedience of faith" (Rom. 1:5; 16:26). It has been said many times that angels are not allowed to preach the gospel—only Christians. The salient question is: Are we going to be obedient to the command of Jesus?

The Key to Church Growth

Knute Rockne was one of the greatest football coaches who ever lived. In his 13 years as head coach at Notre Dame, his teams won 105 games, lost 12, and tied 5. That is an outstanding 85.7% winning percentage. Other coaches knew that he never had a secret practice. In fact, he sometimes would put up a sign for visitors that read, "Secret practice today, come and bring your notebooks." One time an Army scout missed a train connection and did not get to see the Notre Dame game he was to cover. Rockne found out about the Army scout and sent him the plays he planned to use against the West Pointers. He explained his action by saying, "It isn't the play that wins, it is the execution." All great coaches agree. Championship teams are made by majoring on the fundamentals—blocking and tackling. Occasionally a team may win a game with a trick or gimmick. But, they will not be a consistent winner that way.

Great churches are built the same way—by majoring on the basics. The fundamentals for Church Growth are: intense studying of the Bible, effective teaching and preaching, praying, visiting, loving, inviting people into our homes, etc. Nothing will ever replace these basic fundamental concepts! Occasionally one may hear of a minister seeking to build a congregation by promoting some spectacular event or gimmick. It is true that these may succeed for a while but seldom do the results last. People soon get wise to gimmicks. The trouble with the spectaculars is that one must continually try to out-do himself by searching for a more spectacular thing to do next. There is no limit how strong a congregation can become when the leadership strives to build on the basics. Remember, the secret is not in the play, it is the execution. An exciting, spiritual, growing church is not built upon some newfangled idea that no one ever thought of before. A church grows by doing the basics and doing them very well! The *USA Today* magazine reported for the period 1995 to 2004, the seven mainline Protestant denominations fell 7.4% while the more conservative churches grew 11.4%. **Churches of Christ need to wake up and realize that we do not have to change our theology and become liberal to grow.**

Using the Work of Peter Drucker

Peter Drucker was a management/leadership guru. He was respected world-wide for his knowledge. He wrote about 50 books on leadership before his death.

Over a 40 year period, the Methodists lost many members. They decided to hire Drucker to examine the cause and what could be done to stop this decline. After a long period of research and study, he gave four simple but major points. We can learn from his analysis of the Methodists. Here are the four points:

(1) **Expect a lot from churchgoers.** Typically, churches that expect a lot find that people rise to meet those expectations. If you demand a lot, you will get a lot. This is a teacher concept used in public schools that really is effective. We need to stress Hebrews 10:25 without apology. We need to stress being like Jesus (1 John 2:6; 1 Pet. 2:21). Jesus went to study God's word every week (Luke 4:16--"as his custom was"). Christians who do not attend Bible School regularly and faithfully (without a valid reason) do not really love God (John 14:15-24; 1 John 2:3-6; 5:3; 2 John 6).

(2) **Expect transformed lives.** This will be demonstrated in attendance, giving, and involvement with the work of the church. Jesus said, "So because thou art lukewarm, and neither hot nor cold, I will spew thee out of my mouth" (Rev. 3:16). Jesus also said, "He that is not with me is against me; and he that gathereth not with me scattereth abroad" (Matt. 12:30).

(3) **Address spiritual needs.** We must put a focus on spiritual needs. The Country Club serves a function but it does not address spiritual needs. God is a holy God (Lev. 19:2) and He expects His children to be holy (1 Pet. 1:15-16). Hebrews 12:14 says, "Without holiness no man shall see the

Lord." We are told to add to our faith the Christian graces: virtue, knowledge, self-control, patience, godliness, brotherly kindness, and love (2 Pet. 1:5-11).

(4)   **Do not apologize for a distinctive belief system.** Some of our brethren have run away from this. In a Bible class at Southern Hills Church of Christ in Abilene, Texas the elder/teacher asked the class, "What do you say when you are asked what church are you a member of?" I responded, "Tell them you are a member of the only church you read about in the New Testament. There is only one church in the New Testament." The elder/teacher was filled with horror and dismay at my answer. He definitely did not like what I said and rejected it. It was obvious he did not believe in the unique, distinctive identity of the New Testament church!

Churches that are growing today have a distinctive belief system. The Mormons and Jehovah's Witnesses have a distinctive belief system and they are growing. Of course they are wrong in their theology. There is a great lesson we need to learn here. The lesson is: It is a big mistake to water down our theology! In the first place, such action is sinful! Secondly, it will not promote real growth of the church. Ed Wharton said, "Once you lose your distinctive message, you lose your evangelistic zeal." He is right! Stafford North wrote, "It is also clear that churches moving away from stronger doctrinal teaching are tending to decline while those seeking to move closer to Scripture are growing."

The Assessment of Others

Dr. Jeff Ray was a Baptist professor at Southwestern Baptist Theological Seminary in Fort Worth, Texas. In the 1960's he wrote an article about the Churches of Christ that was published in the Fort Worth Star Telegram newspaper. Listen very carefully to what he said about us:

> They, both preachers and people, do stick to the Bible. They definitely believe something and know what they believe. They never miss an opportunity to express it. They defend and boldly speak to propagate their views on every part of the ground. I wish that all our religious bodies could see the wisdom of adopting that method of propagating their faith. Spreading yourself out so thin that you can hold nothing and propagate nothing that people of other faiths could not adopt is a hopeless method of promoting Christ's cause.

Dr. Ray was in essence stating that at one time we were proud of our distinctive belief system. We need to teach and preach without apology there is only one church in the New Testament--even if some brethren, like the elder at Southern Hills, do not like it or agree with it! The apostasy started in the eldership (Acts 20:28-32) so it should not surprise us that we have ignorant and unfaithful elders.

Wayne Dehoney was at one time the President of the Southern Baptist convention. He made a significant statement concerning Churches of Christ in his 1971 book *Set the Church Afire.* This was his assessment of us on page 30:

> A closer look at the Churches of Christ would hardly reveal that their brand of religion is on the downgrade! This fast-growing group is one of the most potent and evangelistic forces in this country . . . A profile of their faith and practice contradicts practically every 'solid conclusion' by the authorities of the main-line denominational establishments about the renewal the church must experience to survive. The Churches of Christ are anti-ecumenical in their theology, autonomous and democratic in the their congregational practices without any semblance of denominational superstructure; they have a rigid Biblical theology, with a strong emphasis of Bible preaching and Bible teaching; they make rigid and moral and ethical demands on their members in such matters as social drinking; they are not 'social action' oriented; they have a 'Messianic complex' about being the true people of God and the true church! . . . And they are growing rapidly.

Notice Dehoney points out that in 1971 we had a "Messianic complex about being the true people of God and the true church!" Then he adds, "And they are growing rapidly." In simple terms we were known as a people who had a distinctive belief system. What happened when we held to that theology? We grew and grew! **Today some brethren want to change to attract potential converts and help the church grow. But, why change what has worked so well? Why water down our theology when strong Bible teaching and** preaching brought about tremendous growth? It is absolute foolishness to change what works when we know God approves. The bottom line must always be what does God think!

The Assessment of Our Brethren

The highly respected Furman Kearley wrote, "One of the most frequent topics of conversation in the church setting today is, 'Why are we not growing?' The most basic and correct answer is that we are not preaching the Gospel as extensively and effectively as we must in order for people to know the vision of God's will and what to do to be saved." Today many Christians believe Kearley is right! Wayne Dehoney acknowledged that in 1971 we had "a strong emphasis of Bible preaching and Bible teaching." Because of that emphasis, we were known as the fastest growing religious body in America. Sadly, unfortunately, that strong emphasis of Bible teaching is non-existent in too many of our churches.

When Clem Thurman moved from Abilene to Fort Worth in the early 1970's he told me, "Out of 12 churches that I visited, I only found one preacher who preached the Bible." In 1988, I went back to the ACU Homecoming where I ate at the preacher's breakfast. I set across from Dr. Speck. Dr. Speck told me that he was teaching a freshman Old Testament Bible class. He asked the class, "How many knew the Old Testament story about Daniel and his three friends?" He told me, "Out of 60 students, only 2 raised their hands." He said, "John when you were here in 1968 out of 60 students only two would not have known the story." What's the point? We as a brotherhood have not taught the Bible to our young people! And now, we are reaping the consequences of weak Bible teaching and weak Bible preaching! In 2005, I had four months to visit churches and evaluate sermons by different preachers. What I heard from too many preachers were sermons with no Bible emphasis. Sad! I observed that the larger the church--the less Bible was used in the sermon.

We must learn that pop-psychology and feel-good sermons will not promote the growth of the Lord's Church. We need strong in-depth Bible teaching--not fluff or chaff! Hosea 4:6 states, "My people are destroyed for a lack of knowledge." What was true in Hosea's day is also true today! The Bible must be the center of our teaching and preaching. Jesus said, "Man shall not live by bread alone but by every word that proceedeth out of the mouth of God" (Matt. 4:4). Peter said, "If any man speaketh, let him speak as the oracles of God" (1 Pet. 4:11). James 1:21 states, "Receive with meekness the implanted word which is able to save your souls." Paul said, "And now I commend you to God, and to the word of his grace, which is able to build you up, and to give you the inheritance among all them that are sanctified" (Acts 20:32).

The Bottom Line for Church Growth

The bottom line for church growth is that God is more concerned with righteousness than numbers. Yes, God wants the church to grow numerically. Every number represents a soul that will live in eternity. To minimize numbers is to minimize souls—which is foolish and ridiculous. God "is not willing that any should perish but that all should come to repentance" (2 Pet. 3:9). God "would have all men to be saved and come to the knowledge of the truth" (1 Tim. 2:4).

How many were saved from the flood? Eight. Why? Because they were righteous. Genesis 6:9 states, "Noah was a righteous man." How many were saved form Sodom and Gomorrah? Less than 10. Why? Those saved from destruction were righteous. 2 Peter 2:7 calls Lot "righteous Lot." How many will be saved on the Day of Judgment? "Few." Read Matthew 7:13-14. One time I quoted Matthew 7:13-14 to a lady and she replied, "I disagree." She was disagreeing with Jesus-- not me. This was His teaching not mine. To disagree with Jesus is the height of foolishness (Matt. 7:24-27).

Who is acceptable to God today? Acts 10:35 states, "In every nation he that feareth him, and worketh righteousness, is acceptable to him." What does it mean to fear God? **In Genesis 22:12 we learn that to obey God regardless of the command is what it means to "fear" Him.** Even though we may not like the command or agree with it, we must be obedient. Jesus "became unto all them that obey him the author of eternal salvation" (Heb. 5:9). Who is righteous? 1 John 3:7 says, "He that doeth righteousness is righteous." What is righteousness? Psalms 119:172 says, "All thy commandments are righteousness." God wants us righteous, faithful, and obedient. As the prophet Samuel said many years ago, "Behold, to obey is better than sacrifice" (1 Sam. 15:22). It is more important to obey God than to give Him what you want to give Him. **It is more important for the Church of Christ to be** righteous than to seek big numbers at the expense of being righteous.

Conclusion

"Change" is in the air. The question we must ask is: "Change from what to what?" Why should we change from what has worked? Why should we change to that which God will not accept? Wisdom demands we reject changes that depart from God's will. Nadab and Abihu offered "strange fire" unto the Lord and were destroyed (Lev. 10:1-2). Let us not make the same mistake. **Peter said, "We must obey God rather than men" (Acts 5:29).** The apostle John wrote, "As for you, let that abide in you which ye heard from the beginning. If that which ye heard from the beginning abide in you, ye also shall abide in the Son, and in the Father. And this is the promise which he promised us, even the life eternal" (1 John 2:24-25). **Paul said, "Hold the pattern" (2 Tim. 1:13) and "Hold the teachings" (2 Thess. 2:15).** Today, many are leaving a worship directed by God and are advocating a departure from a "Thus saith the Lord" attitude. However, we must demand scriptural authority (Col. 3:17). Now is the time to speak out against all sinful "will-worship." Paul said, "Hold the teachings"— he did not say to change them! **It will never be right or appropriate to change what God has legislated and required in His word. From this there can be absolutely no wavering, no vacillation, and no compromise! Period!**

For Thought or Discussion

1. Does the seed of the kingdom plant itself?
2. How does the Holy Spirit work in salvation?
3. What are the fundamentals that promote real church growth? What do you think is most important?
4. What four points did Peter Drucker give that can help us grow? Discuss each one.
5. What did Wayne Dehoney say about Churches of Christ?
6. What did Furman Kearley say about why we are not growing? Do you agree? Why?
7. What does Hosea 4:6 teach?
8 What is the bottom line of church growth?
9. What does Matthew 7:13-14 teach?
10. What does it mean to "fear God?"
11. Was it always easy for Jesus to obey the Father? Will it always be easy for you and me to obey the Father?
12. How did Jesus learn obedience? (Heb. 5:7-9) What does that say to you and me?
13. Who is righteous?
14. What does Acts 5:29 teach?
15. (True or False) We should change our theology to attract the unchurched. Why?

3

Returning to God?

The *Newsweek* magazine, December 17, 1990, cover read "And the Children Shall Lead Them--Young Americans Return to God." This article deals with the generation of the 1960's. These people admitted they did not have any use for God or religion. But now, they have grown up, married, and have children. The article says, "At one time or another, roughly two-thirds of baby boomers dropped out of organized religion. But in recent years, more than one third of the dropouts have returned . . . The biggest group of returnees (about 60%) are married with children." Now these boomers see a need for their children to have a solid spiritual foundation, a spiritual center, and spiritual training. Their children are leading the parents to return to church. The article states, "The return to religion is fueled by the boomers' experiences of becoming parents--and the realization that children need a place where they can learn solid values and make friends with peers who share them." They also are looking for a meaning to life. The article also states, "That search for meaning is a powerful motivation to return to the pews. In the throes of a midlife re-evaluation, Ecclesiastes--'A time for everything under heaven'--is suddenly relevant." Timothy Galligan said, "Boomers are looking for a religious experience that makes sense of their lives and gives them some answers to their questions." However, the big problem is the type of church they are looking for. They are not looking for the church of the New Testament, the church that Jesus died for, the church that Jesus is going to take to heaven! The boomers' are looking for a church that is convenient, entertaining, one that does not point out sin in their life, one that does not preach a list of do's and don'ts, one that offers support--not salvation, and one that offers help not holiness. Sociologist Wade Clark Roof of the University of California informs us, "They inspect congregations as if they were restaurants and leave if they find nothing to their taste. Participation follows not out of duty or obligation usually but if it fits their needs. They don't convert--they choose."

The apostle Paul wrote, "Preach the word; be urgent in season, out of season; reprove, rebuke, exhort, with all longsuffering and teaching. For the time will come when they will not endure the sound doctrine; but, having itching ears, will heap to themselves teachers after their own lusts; and will turn aside their ears from the truth, and turn aside unto fables" (2 Tim. 4:2-4). Solomon wrote a long time ago, "There is a way which seemeth right unto a man; but the end thereof are the ways of death" (Prov. 14:12).

Nail this point down--The Church of Christ should not, cannot, and must not compete with the world in the realm of entertainment. The function of the Lord's Church is not to entertain or provide physical recreation. Too many of our brethren go to a church with the attitude--they want to be entertained. But, let us stop and ask ourselves--where is our strength? It is in providing something for people they cannot get anywhere else! We are to provide spiritual food for the souls of men. We can provide something that the entertainment world, the recreational world and the country club very simply cannot! The Church of Christ is not to be a glorified county club and Six Flags combined.

The Main Purpose of the Church

Before Jesus left this world He said, "All authority hath been given unto me in heaven and on earth. **Go** ye therefore, and **make disciples** of all the nations, **baptizing** them into the name of the Father and of the Son and of the Holy Spirit: **teaching** them to observe all things whatsoever I commanded you: and lo, I am with you always, even unto the end of the world" (Matt. 28:18-20). In this Great Commission we find the main function of the church--"make disciples." There are three participles in Greek (go, baptizing, and teaching) that modify the main verb "make disciples." Jesus told Peter three times if you love me, **"feed my sheep"** (John 21:15-17). When Paul left the Ephesian elders he said, "Take heed unto yourselves, in which the Holy Spirit hath made you bishops, **to feed the church of the Lord** which he purchased with his own blood" (Acts 20:28). The leaders of the Lord's Church are to teach and preach the word of God to provide the brethren with the spiritual nourishment they need to grow spiritually (1 Pet. 2:2; James1:21; Col. 1:28). Paul wrote, "Speaking truth in love, we may grow up in all things into him, who is the head, even Christ" (Eph. 4:15).

To Whom or What Do We Listen?

Job said, "I have treasured up the words of his (i.e. God's) mouth more than my necessary food" (Job 23:12). Is this our attitude? Do we desire the word of God more than physical food or entertainment? If not, why not? The boomer generation is not concerned with a "Thus saith the Lord." Their attitude in returning to God is worthless! For the majority of people today, a group affirmation of self is at the top of the agenda. Many do not want or seek an authoritative guide for their lives. God told the Israelites in Jeremiah's day, "No man repenteth him of his wickedness, saying, What have I done? Every one turneth to his course, as a horse that rusheth headlong in the battle" (Jer. 8:6). The expression "turneth to his course" means that each person did what he thought not what God said! It is significant that Jeremiah said, "The priests bear rule by their means" (Jer. 5:31)—not by God's means! Judges 17:6 states, "In those days there was no king in Israel: every man did that which was right in his own eyes." Notice they were doing that which they thought was right in their own eyes--not God's eyes! God said, "For my thoughts are not your thoughts, neither are your ways my ways" (Isa. 55:8). Jeremiah wrote, "O Jehovah, I know that the way of man is not in himself; it is not in man that walketh to direct his steps" (Jer. 10:23). We must come to understand that we are to listen to God through His Word and no one else! Psalms 119:105 states, "Thy word is a lamp unto my feet, and light unto my path." Jesus said, "Man shall not live by bread alone, but by every word that proceedeth out of the mouth of God" (Matt. 4:4).

God Is The Ruler—Not Man

In this article William Schulz, president of the Unitarian Universalist Association, said, "Each individual is the ultimate source of authority." Brethren, this is heresy of the highest order! We do not make up our own rules on what is right or wrong! God does! When Moses came down from Mount Sinai, he came down with Ten Commandments--not Ten Suggestions! Over and over in the Book of Deuteronomy God tells the Israelites if you obey Me, I will bless you. If you disobey Me, I will curse you. We must learn to seek to please God not ourselves. We are not in charge! Listen to these warnings: "Lean not upon thine own understanding" (Prov. 3:5); "Be not wise in thine own eyes" (Prov. 3:7); "Cease from thine own wisdom" (Prov. 23:4); "He that trusteth in his own heart is a fool" (Prov. 28:26); "Woe unto them that are wise in their own eyes, and prudent in their own sight!" (Isa. 5:21). The word "woe" means "great grief and sorrow and misery are coming upon you." Jesus said, "He that rejecteth me, and receiveth not my sayings, hath one that judgeth him: the word which I spake, the same shall judge him on the last day" (John 12:48). One day, we will all be judged by the truth of the word of God (Rom. 2:2; John 17:17; Rev. 20:12).

Humanists teach that each individual is his own ultimate authority. However, the Bible teaches God is the Authority and Creator and we are the creatures. When men try to be God--they sin! Remember Satan tempted Eve in the Garden of Eden and said if you will eat of the forbidden tree, you will be as God. Of course this was a lie! Satan is working today! Satan is trying to get people to believe that they themselves determine right and wrong. Do you want a preacher to tell what you want to hear or what you need to hear?

Christianity Is a Religion of Faith

Hebrews 11:6 states, "Without **faith** it is impossible to be well-pleasing unto him; for he that cometh to God must believe that he is, and that he is a rewarder of them that seek after him." We "walk by **faith**" (2 Cor. 5:7); "Live by **faith**" (Gal. 3:11); and are "Justified by **faith**" (Rom. 5:1). Faith is "unto the saving of the soul" (Heb. 10:39). Peter said that "The end of our **faith**" is "the salvation of your souls" (1 Pet. 1:9). Paul wrote, "For by grace have ye been saved through **faith**" (Eph. 2:8). Jesus said, "Be thou **faithful** unto death, and I will give thee the crown of life" (Rev. 2:10). Romans 1:17 teaches that our salvation starts in faith and ends in faith. John wrote, "And this is the victory that overcometh the world, even our **faith**" (1 John 5:4). But the very important question comes—How does faith come? Romans 10:17 states, **"Faith cometh by hearing, and hearing by the word of God."** John 20:30-31 states, "Many other signs therefore did Jesus in the presence of the disciples, which are not written in this book: but **these are written that ye might believe that Jesus is the Christ, the Son of God; and that believing ye may have life in his name**." Jesus prayed, "Neither for these only do I pray, but for them also that **believe** on me **through their (i.e. the apostles) word**" (John 17:20). **Our faith will take us to heaven but our faith comes through the word of God. This is why the Lord's church must preach the Bible--not pop psychology, not the social gospel, not I'm ok you're ok, not a feel**

good religion. We must preach and teach the truth! This demands that sometimes we point out sin in peoples' lives. Holy Scripture is crystal clear--unless people repent, they are lost into an eternal hell of fire where there are no chances of getting out (Luke 13:3; Luke 16:19-31; Acts 17:30-31; John 8:24). Paul said, "And now I commend you to God, and the word of his grace, which is able to build you up, and to give you the inheritance among all them that are sanctified" (Acts 20:32).

The article stated, "For earlier generations, the service was a stitch in time to hear the familiar word of God and to get right with the Lord. Those Sundays are long gone." But, they should not be gone! God's people must demand that the word of God be preached even if some brethren don't like it, even if some brethren leave, even if some brethren hold their contributions and refuse to give because they do not like what is being preached. If the preacher is fired for preaching the truth, God be praised. Paul wrote in 1 Corinthians 11:19, "For there must also be factions among you, that they that are approved may be made manifest among you." In other words, when a split or division occurs among brethren, the reason for the split is made known. The righteous will be vindicated by not going along with the anti-Scriptural practices and beliefs of the liberals! Jeremiah 6:16 states, **"Thus saith Jehovah, Stand ye in the ways and see, and ask for the old paths, where is the good way; and walk therein, and ye shall find rest for your souls." This is what we must do—"Ask for the Old Paths."** Today, too many Churches of Christ are leaving the old paths. They preach to make people feel good instead of making them feel guilty so they will see the need to repent. **The Bible still says, "Godly sorrow worketh repentance unto salvation" (2 Cor. 7:10).** Shame is a good thing to get people to repent. If people do not feel the pains of guilt and remorse and shame, they will never repent and thus they never will be saved. Thus, we need to preach the truth to make people feel the guilt and remorse of sin! God told the Jews many years ago, "Thou refusedst to be ashamed" (Jer. 3:3). Zephaniah 3:5 states, "The unjust knoweth no shame."

The Importance of Sin

The article states, "In their efforts to accommodate, many clergy have simply airbrushed sin out of their language." One man wrote a book entitled *What Ever Happened to Sin?* Some elders in the Church of Christ have told their preachers do not preach on sin because that will drive people away. Drive them where? Hell number 2? Hell number 3? Hell number 4, etc??? If they are living in sin, they are going to hell unless they repent (Luke 13:3). Some preachers have banished hellfire and damnation sermons. Many brethren do not want a preacher to make them feel bad or preach on hell or preach on sin. We are told by some to accept people as they are without any sort of do's and don'ts. This is a far cry from the Old Testament prophets and apostles and how they preached. We commit an eternal mistake if we minimize sin. Preachers commit sin and will have to answer to God if they do not warn people living in sin (cf. Ezek. 33:8-9).

Sin separates man and God (Isa. 59:1-2). God told wicked Judah, "Your iniquities have turned away these things (i.e. blessings), and your sins have withholden good from you" (Jer. 5:25). Nehemiah said that God set kings over us "because of our sins" and as a result "we are in great distress" (Neh. 9:37). The apostle Paul talked being "dead through our trespasses" (Eph. 2:5). Sin causes one to be dead spiritually. Sin that is unforgiven will cause one to lose their soul in an eternal hell of fire (where the worm dieth not and the fire is not quenched--Mark 9:47-48). Sin must not be taken lightly. Our eternal souls are at stake.

When Mary was with child of the Holy Spirit, it was announced, "And she shall bring forth a son; and thou shalt call his name Jesus; for it is he that shall save his people from their sins" (Matt. 1:21). In Mark 10:45 Jesus said, "For the Son of Man also came not to be ministered unto, but to minister and give his life a ransom for many." Hebrews 9:26 states, "But now once at the end of the ages hath he been manifested to put away sin by the sacrifice of himself." It is through the blood of Jesus that sin is atoned for. We have redemption through the blood of Jesus (Eph. 1:7). Jesus "made peace through the blood of his cross" (Col. 1:20). John wrote, "Unto him that loveth us, and loosed us from our sins by his blood" (Rev. 1:5). We are reconciled to God "through the cross" (Eph. 2:16).

On the Day of Pentecost, Peter pointed out twice the sins of the Jews. In Acts 2:23 he said, "Ye by the hand of lawless men did crucify and slay." In Acts 2:36 he said, "Let all the house of Israel therefore know assuredly, that God hath made him both Lord and Christ, this Jesus whom ye crucified." Notice their response. Acts 2:37 says, "Now when they heard this, they were pricked in their heart, and said unto Peter and the rest of the apostles, Brethren, what shall we do?" Wouldn't it be great today if people had that attitude? If a preacher preaches the word of God and the word of God points out something wrong in your life, realize the preacher is doing you a favor. Paul wrote, "So then am I become your enemy, by telling you the truth?" (Gal. 4:16). Proverbs 9:8 states, "Reprove not a scoffer, lest he hate thee: Reprove a wise man, and he will love thee." If you get on the scales to weigh yourself, don't get mad at the scales, they are just revealing truth.

God's People Have Suffered for Standing for Righteousness and Truth!

Noah's sermons did not say, "Something good is going to happen to you today." He "condemned the world" (Heb. 11:7) by being a preacher of righteousness. Isaiah, according to tradition, was put into a hollow log and sawed in half. Hebrews 11:37 teaches some "were sawn asunder." Jeremiah was not put into a dungeon for preaching, "I'm okay, you're okay." He was put into a dungeon because he cried out against the sins of God's people like adultery, idolatry, lying, cheating, etc. When John the Baptist preached in the desert, he did not say, "Smile God loves you!" Instead he said, "Oh generation of vipers, who hath warned you to flee from the wrath to come" (Matt. 3:7). John the Baptist did not have his head cut off for saying, "Your present marital state is okay. God accepts you right where you are." He was decapitated because he told the king, "It is not lawful for you to have your brother's wife" (Matt. 14:4). Jesus called the Pharisees "blind guides, fools, whited sepulchers, full of dead men's bones, serpents, generation of vipers." They did not like it and crucified Him. Stephen was stoned to death because he preached the truth to the Jews and they did not like it (Acts 7). Paul was stoned, beaten five times, shipwrecked three times, often in hunger and thirst, and often in cold and nakedness--all because he preached the truth and people did not like it and sought to kill him (2 Cor. 11:24-27). Jesus taught that there may be times that we might have to be "at variance" with our own family because we stand for the truth (Matt. 10:34-39). Read very carefully Hebrews 11:32-40 and discover the price that God's people paid for their faithfulness. It is an eye opener! Jesus said, "Woe unto you, when all men speak well of you!" (Luke 6:26). The point is if you stand for the truth--expect opposition. **God's people have always been in the minority and should expect to be in the minority.**

The Wrath of God

Many ignorant people say the God of the Old Testament is a God of wrath, anger, and hate--but the God of the New Testament is a God of love, mercy, grace, and kindness. This is pure ignorance. The Old Testament teaches the love of God (cf. Deut. 4:37; 6:4-6; 7:7-8; 10:15; 33:3; Jer. 31:3; Isa. 63: 9; etc.). The Bible teaches very clearly that God does not change (Mal. 3:6; Heb.13:8; James 1:17). It is also blind ignorance when anyone chooses to ignore the clear teaching of Scripture. Paul in Romans 11:22 taught "the goodness and severity of God." John 3:36 states, "He that believeth on the Son hath eternal life; but he that obeyeth not the Son shall not see life, but **the wrath of God** abideth on him." Paul wrote, "For **the wrath of God** is revealed from heaven against all ungodliness and unrighteousness of men" (Rom. 1:18). Paul also talked about **"wrath"** coming on the impenitent and disobedient (Rom. 2:5-9). Ephesians 5:6 states, "For because of these things cometh **the wrath of God** upon the sons of disobedience." Jesus taught "eternal punishment" (Matt. 25:46). Paul also wrote about "eternal destruction" (2 Thess. 1:9) that will come upon those who "obey not the gospel of our Lord Jesus."

God uses the fear of His wrath to get people on the right path. Proverbs 16:6 says, "And by the fear of Jehovah, men depart from evil." 2 Corinthians 5:11 says, "Knowing therefore the fear of the Lord, we persuade men." Hebrews 10:31 reads, "It is a fearful thing to fall into the hands of the living God." Hebrews 12:29 states, "For our God is a consuming fire." When Paul preached to Felix about "the judgment to come, Felix was terrified" (Acts 24:25). Why? Because Paul put the fear of God in him. Paul preached the seriousness of the judgment to come and the need to be ready for it! This is the kind of preaching we need today! **Regardless of what kind of preaching people want, those faithful to God will preach the tough truth of Scripture that sin is sin. We will preach that unrepentant sin will cost one their soul in an eternal hell of fire! This is not popular but it is biblical.**

Conclusion

We are not to create a church of your choice. We are not to preach to please men (Gal. 1:10). We must preach **the wrath of God** in order to get men to repent!

If obedience to God causes the numbers in our Churches to go down, so be it! What we must do is "ask for the old paths" (Jer. 6:16) and follow them even if the majority say "we will not walk therein" (Jer. 6:16). Those Americans who are returning to God to find a church of their choice that preaches false doctrine are making an eternal mistake. Jesus only died for one church. Jesus only built one church. Jesus will only save one church--His church--not the church of your choice.

For Thought or Discussion

1. What kind of church are the boomers looking for?
2. What is the main purpose of the church? How is that done?
3. Explain "The priests bear rule by their means."
4. What did William Schulz say? Do you agree? Why?
5. Explain "Lean not upon thine own understanding."
6. Discuss Proverbs 3:5; 3:7; 23:4; 28:26; Isa. 5:21.
7. How does one obtain faith? Scripture?
8. What does Acts 20:32 teach?
9. What was the cure for sin from Jeremiah 6:16?
10. Discuss the problem of sin.
11. From Hebrews 11: 32-40 what is the price for obedience?
12. Should the wrath of God be preached?
13. What does Luke 6:26 teach?
14. How should people return to God?
15. (True or False) The Old Testament does not teach the love of God.
16. (True or False) Preachers should not preach on sin causing people to feel bad.

17. What does 1 John 5:4 teach?
18. (True or False) God's people have always been in the minority and should always expect to be in the minority. Why?

4

Restoring the New Testament Church

Every church has its own peculiar plea. The peculiar plea of the Church of Christ is let us go back to the Bible and the Bible alone as the final authority in all religious matters. It is the same as the plea: **"Ask for the old paths."** Jesus said, "Man shall not live by bread alone, but by every word that proceedeth out of the mouth of God" (Matt. 4:4). Peter said, "If any man speaketh, let him speak as the oracles of God" (1 Pet. 4:11). Paul wrote that we are "not to go beyond the things which are written" (1 Cor. 4:6). According to Revelation 20:12 we will be "judged by the things which were written in the books" (i.e. the books of the Bible). The Word will judge us on the last day (John 12:48). Therefore, let us go back to the word of God as the full and final authority! Let us throw away the Manuals, Discipline Books, Creed Books, Confessions of Faith and follow only the Bible. The Bible teaches very clearly that we are commanded not to add to or subtract from God's word (cf. Deut. 4:2; 12:32; Prov. 30:5-6; Matt. 4:4; 1 Cor. 4:6; 14:37; Gal. 3:15; Rev. 22:18-19).

The Establishment of the Church (Kingdom)

Isaiah 2:2-3 prophesies that in the latter days (i.e. the last days of the Jewish nation) the mountain of Jehovah's house shall be established on the top of the mountains and shall be exalted above the hills (this is the establishment of God's kingdom/church) and all nations shall flow unto it (the command Jesus gave was to "make disciples of all the nations"--Matt. 28:19--and to "preach the gospel to every creature"--Mark 16:15-16). This mountain is called "the house of the God of Jacob" (the church is called the house of God—1 Tim. 3:15). Isaiah says that the word of Jehovah would go forth from Jerusalem (Luke 24:46-47 records the fulfillment of this in that repentance and remission of sins should be preached in his name unto all the nations, beginning in Jerusalem).

Daniel 2:44 states, "And in the days of those kings shall the God of heaven set up a kingdom which shall never be destroyed." The "mountain" of Isaiah 2 is the "kingdom" of Daniel 2. Studying Daniel 2 we discover that "the days of those kings" were the Roman kings (cf. Luke 2:1 and Luke 3:1). The main question that must be asked is: Has God done this or this a yet to be fulfilled prophecy? I demand an answer to this question!

The kingdom of heaven was "at hand" during the days of John the Baptist (Matt. 3:2), Jesus (Matt. 4:17), the twelve (Matt. 10:7), and the seventy (Luke 10:1, 9). The expression "at hand" means close by, right around the corner. This is made clear by two key verses. In Mark 1:15 Jesus is preaching, "**The time is fulfilled**, and the kingdom of God is at hand: repent ye, and believe in the gospel." Notice Jesus said, **"The time is fulfilled!"** What time? The time of the prophesied kingdom is close by; it is right around the corner. **In Mark 9:1 we read, "And he said unto them, Verily I say unto you, there are some here of them that stand by, who shall in no wise taste of death, till they see the kingdom of God come with power."** The only conclusion we can come to is that the kingdom of God was going to be set up and established in the lifetime of those who heard Jesus preach! Some liberals say that Jesus made a mistake in Mark 9:1. Conservative scholarship absolutely denies that! The power was coming when the Holy Spirit would come (Acts 1:8). In Acts 2:1-4, the Holy Spirit came, therefore the power came and the kingdom also came into existence.

Please read very carefully pages 199-201 in the book *The Word Was God* by John Hobbs to see that the Kingdom and the Church are the same entity. Jesus used the terms church and kingdom interchangeably in Matthew 16:18-19. Acts 5:11 says, "And great fear came upon the whole church." Therefore, the church was established sometime between Matthew 16 and Acts 5:11. The Bible teaches that the church/kingdom was established on the Day of Pentecost in Acts 2. There are many passages which teach the kingdom is in existence (cf. Col. 1:13, Rev. 1:9; etc.). **Those preachers who preach that the kingdom is yet to be established are teaching false doctrine! Mark 9:1 cannot be annulled.**

How Many Churches Are There?

The New Testament clearly teaches that there is only "one body" (cf. Eph. 4:4; Col. 3:15; 1 Cor. 12:12, 13, 20; Rom. 12:4, 5). Paul wrote, "And he is the head of the body, the church" (Col. 1:18). In Ephesians 1:22-23 he wrote, "The church, which is his body." If the body = the church and the church = the body and there is only "one body," how many churches are there? The answer is one! This is not blind arrogance. This is the teaching of the New Testament. Some say we are being narrow-minded. But, brethren wait a minute. Truth is narrow-minded. Jesus Himself taught there is only "one flock" (John 10:16).

In Matthew 16:18 Jesus said, "I will build my church" (note not churches) and "the gates of Hades will not prevail against it' (note not them). Some preachers have prayed, "God I thank you that there are so many churches so that one can join the church of his choice." But, I want to ask a simple question. Did Jesus die and establish His church or the church of your choice? Jesus only built one church (Matt. 16:18). Jesus only died for one church (Eph. 5:25). Jesus only purchased one church with his blood (Acts 20:28). Jesus will only save one church (Eph. 5:23). All churches are not the same. They teach conflicting doctrines. Ephesians 4:5 teaches there is "one baptism." Today, the majority of churches in America does not teach the "one baptism" of Christianity and are therefore not teaching the truth! Ephesians 4:5 also teaches there is only "one faith" (i.e. one system of Christian doctrine on how to be right with God). And yet, you can drive down the streets of many towns in America and find that each church has its own faith system. Since there is only "one faith," someone has to be wrong!

The Church Was Not and Is Not a Denomination

A denomination is a part of something. The Church that was established on the Day of Pentecost was not part of anything. It was the whole. It was not broken up into different faiths, different baptisms, different types of worship, different religious bodies. The apostle Paul wrote, "All the churches of Christ salute you" (Rom. 16:16). Here we find the biblical name for the church of the New Testament. It is "the Church of Christ." It is the Church that belongs to Christ (Acts 20:28) and is owned by Christ (1 Cor. 6:19-20). Psalms 127:1 states, "Except Jehovah build the house, they labor in vain that build it." Jesus said, "Every plant which my heavenly Father planted not, shall be rooted up" (Matt. 15:13). If a church is not following the New Testament in the plan of salvation, worship, organization, etc., it will be rooted up and destroyed! Again Paul wrote, "Now I beseech you, brethren, mark them that are causing the divisions and occasions of stumbling, contrary to the doctrine which ye learned: and turn away from them" (Rom. 16:17). If someone preaches a doctrine "contrary to the doctrine which ye learned," Paul says "mark" him and "turn away from him." This verse clearly teaches that there is a right way that must be followed, and if one departs from this right way, he is to be marked and avoided. Paul asked the question, "Is Christ divided?" (1 Cor. 1:13). The answer is a resounding "No!" Christ is not divided up into different parts. One is either in Christ, or he is not in Christ. We must teach that there is "one body" and "one faith" and "one baptism" (Eph. 4:4-6). Paul taught that those who are guilty of "divisions"--"shall not inherit the kingdom of God" (Gal. 5:19-21).

The Apostasy/Falling Away Was Predicted

In Acts 20:29-30 Paul prophesied that the apostasy/falling away would start in the eldership. There is a warning here for us today. Just because a person is an elder, that does not mean he is really and truly qualified to be an elder. Also, every decision than an elder decides does not mean it is approved of by God. There are many good elders in our brotherhood, but there are also bad, unqualified elders.

1 Timothy 4:1-3 states, "But the Spirit saith expressly, that in later times some shall fall away from the faith, giving heed to seducing spirits and doctrines of demons, through the hypocrisy of men that speak lies, branded in their own conscience as with a hot iron; forbidding to marry, and commanding to abstain from meats, which God created to be received with thanksgiving by them that believe and know the truth."

2 Thessalonians 2:3-4 states, "For it will not be (i.e. the second coming of Christ) except the falling away come first (i.e. the apostasy), and the man of sin be revealed (i.e. the Pope), the son of perdition, he that opposeth and exalteth himself against all that is called God or is worshipped; so that he that sitteth in the temple of God, setting himself forth as God."

History revealed this departure. The departure from the original pattern was gradual. From among the elders there arose the false doctrine of separating one elder out as "the bishop" with special authority. This is false doctrine because the New Testament teaches one elder does not have more authority than another elder (Acts 20:17-28; 1 Pet. 5:1-4). From the bishop concept came the cardinals. From the cardinals came the Pope (around 606 A.D.). In 250, infant baptism was introduced over strong opposition. In 389, the Catholics initiated the worship of Mary. In 1079, Catholics forbade their priests to marry--a clear violation of 1 Timothy 4. Catholics forbade the eating of meats on Friday--a clear violation of 1 Timothy 4. In 1311, Catholics practiced sprinkling for immersion and calling that baptism. But, the Greek word *baptizo* means immersion. In 1870, Catholics accepted the doctrine of Papal Infallibility. This doctrine says that when the Pope speaks *ex cathedra* (literally-out of the chair) he is speaking for God and cannot sin. The Pope accepts worship which is a violation of Scripture. The New Testament opens with the command "Worship God" (Matt. 4:10) and it closes with the admonition "Worship God" (Rev. 19:10). We are to worship God--not the Pope or Mary or angels or any human being! Peter refused worship (Acts 10:25-26). Paul refused worship (Acts 14:13-18). Good angels refused worship (Rev. 22:8-9).

The Roman Catholic Church changed the name, doctrine, worship, baptism, and practices of the Lord's Church. Gradually, this apostate church took the Bible out of the hands of the common people and chained it to the pulpit. The people were told that they could not understand it by themselves. They were told the priests had to tell them what the Bible means. Again, this was a departure from Scripture. Ephesians 5:17 states, "Wherefore be ye not foolish, but understand what the will of the Lord is." This is a command for every Christian to study and understand the Bible for himself. This is a far cry from Catholic doctrine. This practice brought on what is known in church history as the Dark Ages. From 600-1500 A.D. such false doctrines such as extreme unction, purgatory, transubstantiation, celibacy, indulgences, etc. came into existence. When Martin Luther was serving as a priest in Wittenburg, Germany, John Tetzel came through raising money for the rebuilding of Saint Peter's Cathedral by selling indulgences. This was all Martin Luther could stand. Others followed Luther's lead which led to a break from the Roman Catholic Church.

The Beginning of Denominationalism

Martin Luther, John Calvin, Zwingli and others had been members of the apostate Roman Catholic Church. They sought to reform it. The Reformation Movement produced the Lutheran church, the Presbyterian church, the Methodist church, the Baptist church and others. Unfortunately, these groups held on to many anti-scriptural practices and beliefs not found in Scripture. In simple terms, they were not following the New Testament pattern. Finally, it began to dawn on some that the Reformation Movement had failed.

The Restoration Movement

The Restoration Movement sought to restore the New Testament Church. Just like Josiah initiated a restoration movement in Judah to go back to the word of God and follow it, some sought to do likewise. This is a valid righteous cause! There are some church history scholars who say that the Church of Christ, as you read about in the New Testament, has always existed. In the late 1700's a movement was launched to restore New Testament Christianity. This was much like Josiah's reform. **Today, many believe in the Restoration Movement because it is a biblically valid righteous cause.** Men like Abner Jones, James O'Kelly, Barton W. Stone, Walter Scott, Racoon John Smith, Thomas Campbell, Alexander Campbell, and many others sought to restore New Testament Christianity. Many of these preachers were Methodists, Presbyterians, and Baptists. Their aim was "Let's go back to the Bible" as the full and final authority in all religious matters. They came up with slogans like "The Bible and the Bible Alone" and "Speak Where the Bible Speaks" and "Be Silent Where the Bible Is Silent." I am not following any man. I am following God through the Bible! I recognize that the Bible is the authority--not some man. Nat Cooper said, "Don't accept any man's interpretation of the Bible unless you are prepared to answer for it on the Day of Judgment--because if you do, you will." How true!

Did Alexander Campbell Start the Church of Christ?

Remember from our study of Scripture that the Church was established on the Day of Pentecost in Jerusalem. Many people out of ignorance say that

Alexander Campbell started the Church of Christ. It is matter of historical fact that the Church of Christ (as restored from the New Testament) was already in existence in America at least by 1807! Alexander Campbell did not arrive in America until 1809! Therefore, it is total falsehood to say that Alexander Campbell started the Church of Christ. Why are members of the Church of Christ called Campbellites? It is simply because the lie has been told and re-told so many times that people say Alexander Campbell started the Church of Christ.

There is a point that must be brought out! Today, all conservative Bible-loving preachers of the Church of Christ do not agree with Alexander Campbell on several points. Alexander wrote the infamous "Lunenburg Letters." In these letters Campbell accepted the view that one could be a Christian without being baptized. This doctrine will be dealt with in this book. Conservative preachers vehemently reject this teaching! We also disagree with Campbell's view of the Missionary Society. So, it is pure ignorance to call me and others Campbellites.

The Church Is Not Built on Peter

The Roman Catholic Church claims that the church was built on Peter. They misuse Matthew 16:16-19 to try to prove their doctrine. Jesus said "And I also say unto thee, that thou art Peter, and upon this rock I will build my church." They say "Peter" means "rock" so the church is built on Peter and claim he was the first Pope. This needs further study. The rock is the Greek word *petra*. The word Peter in Greek is *petros*. *Petra* means a large mass of unmovable rock. *Petros* means a small pebble stone. The definition of the words disproves their doctrine. Also, the gender disproves their doctrine. *Petra* is feminine gender and *petros* is masculine gender. Thus, Jesus is saying, Peter you are a he-rock and upon this she-rock I will build my church. The rock was not Peter. The rock was what Peter confessed Jesus to be--Deity (Matt. 16:16). Also, 1 Corinthians 3:11 proclaims Jesus as the foundation of the Church! The authority to bind and loose was also given to the other apostles in Matthew 18:18 not just Peter. However, Peter was given the keys of the kingdom, and he used those keys when he preached the first gospel sermon that infused faith into the hearers and gave the terms of admission into the kingdom--Repent and be Baptized (Acts 2:38).

The Roman Catholic Church tries to find a line of succession of popes back to Peter. They claim Peter was the first Pope. But, we are not interested in trying to find a line of succession. In the first place, church doctrine did not originate with Peter! Jesus told Peter whatever he bound on earth would have already been bound in heaven and whatever he loosed on earth would have already been loosed in heaven. This is the use of the Greek Future Perfect Tense in Matt. 16:19. In other words what Peter and the other apostles taught originated in heaven, not in them!

Seed Reproduces after Its Kind

We are not trying to find a line of succession back to Peter. We are trying to take the seed of the kingdom, which is the word of God (Luke 8:11), and plant it into the lives of people today. In the physical realm, there is an unalterable law that says that seed reproduces after its kind. If you plant a pecan seed, what are going to get? An apple tree? No, you will get a pecan tree! If you plant an apple seed, what are going to get? A peach tree? No, you will get an apple tree! Why? Because seed reproduces after its kind. Suppose I went to Alabama and ate some cantaloupe and brought some cantaloupe seeds home to Texas and planted them. What would I get? Little Hobbses? Of course not! I would get cantaloupes. Why? Because seed reproduces after its kind. Mark this down--Who carries the seed or who brings the seed or who plants the seed has absolutely nothing to do with what the seed produces! Now, in the spiritual realm the seed of the kingdom is the word of God (Luke 8:11). Today, if we plant the seed of the kingdom which is the word of God, we will get Christians and only Christians! The denominational world is not teaching the truth on how to become a Christian! **Saying the sinner's prayer will not save one or make him a Christian. Joel Osteen is dead wrong!**

We have a very popular game in this country called baseball. It is played according to certain rules and regulations. Let us suppose that people were to gradually lose interest in the game and quit playing it. But, let us suppose that 1000 years after people quit playing the game that someone finds a baseball rule book. They start playing the game according to the rule book. Question--Would that be a new game or the old game of baseball restored? If we go back to the New Testament and the New Testament alone (which was the rule book used by the apostles and early Christians) and follow it precisely--adding nothing and taking nothing from it--will we have a new church or the Church of the New Testament restored? I want an answer to that question.

Conclusion

The concept of restoring the New Testament Church is a biblical one. It is a plea for every generation to go back to the Bible and the Bible alone to find out what is binding and permanent and what is free for humans to decide. **It is a plea to: "Ask for the old paths, where is the good way; and walk therein, and ye shall find rest for your souls" (Jer. 6:16).** Admittedly, those in the Churches of Christ are criticized and attacked for being narrow-minded. But, truth is narrow-minded. When we teach the truth of God's word and people do not like it, they have a problem--not us! Remember those in the Bible who suffered because they taught the truth--like Stephen in Acts 7. **The New Testament teaches that simply saying the sinner's prayer does not, cannot, and never will make one a Christian.** Jesus taught that many of his followers are going to be surprised on the Day of Judgment and rejected (Matt. 7:21-23). This fact alone should motivate every one of us to be good, serious minded Bible students.

For Thought or Discussion

1. What does Isaiah 2:2-3 teach?
2. What does Daniel 2:44 teach?
3. What does Mark 1:15 and Mark 9:1 teach?
4. When was the Church established?

5. How many churches, baptisms, faiths are there in the New Testament?
6. Who are we to mark and turn away from? Discuss.
7. Discuss how the Catholics fulfill the predicted falling away/apostasy.
8. What does Ephesians 5:17 teach?
9. Do all Churches of Christ agree with Alexander Campbell on every point?
10. (True or False) Who carries the seed or who brings the seed or who plants the seed has absolutely nothing to do with what the seed produces.
11. Discuss Matthew 16:16-19. What does the Greek Future Perfect Tense tell us in verse 19?
12. (True or False) Saying the sinner's prayer makes one a Christian.
13. What did Josiah do in the Old Testament that provides an example for us?
14. What was Nat Cooper's notable quote? Do you agree? Why?
15. Will many of the followers of Jesus be surprised on the Day of Judgment? Why? What does this truth teach us?
16. Why should the Restoration Movement be pursued today?
17. (True or False) Mark 1:14-15 and 9:1 teach the promised kingdom came in the lifetime of those who heard Jesus preaching.

5

The New Testament Pattern

The plea of Churches of Christ is let us **ask for the old paths** (Jer. 6:16). Let us seek to restore what is right (cf. Josiah). Let us go back to the Bible. Let us go all the way back to the Bible. Let's don't stop half way. Let us throw away the manuals, discipline books, confessions of faith, creed books and follow only God's word. Anything more than the Bible is too much and anything less than the Bible is not enough. When Weldon Bennett was a young man, he joined the Methodist church. Before a public audience, the Methodist preacher asked Weldon, "Do you promise to abide by all the rules and regulations set forth in the Methodist Discipline?" Weldon told me he said yes, but he had never even seen a Methodist Discipline. Eventually, Weldon found the truth and became a preacher and missionary for the Churches of Christ. He was one of my Bible teachers. I had six graduate Bible courses under Weldon.

There Is a Pattern

The apostle Paul told the young preacher Timothy, **"Hold the pattern"** (2 Tim. 1:13). Liberals in our brotherhood say there is no religious pattern to follow. But, this verse is crystal clear. There is a pattern to follow, and we are told to hold to it! Those who deny this are denying the teaching of Scripture. We might question what the pattern is, but we must agree that there is a pattern to follow.

Concerning 2 Timothy 1:13 Ed Wharton wrote, "Clearly, back of this language lies a pattern of sound doctrine which we can 'hold' by practice and teaching. The apostles' words form themselves into distinct doctrines of the Christian system which can be categorized: such as, the law of pardon and induction into the church; the organizational structure of the church; the work; the worship; the discipline of the church; and the Christian life. We are expected to discern these doctrines and to hold them as the pattern for the New Testament church" (*The Church of Christ*, p. 9).

2 Thessalonians 2:15, "Hold the traditions (i.e. teachings) which ye were taught, whether by word, or epistle of ours." Notice that Paul said, "Hold the teachings." We are to hold the teachings of Paul up as our authoritative guide. Jesus gave the apostles authority (Matt. 18:18; Luke 10:16; John 13:20), and that authority extends to the writings of Paul (2 Pet. 3:15-17).

2 Thessalonians 3:6, "Now we command you, brethren, in the name of our Lord Jesus Christ, that ye withdraw yourselves from every brother that walketh disorderly, and not after the tradition which they received of us." Notice Paul taught these Christians a principle that they were to follow.

2 Thessalonians 3:14, "And if any man obeyeth not our word by this epistle, note that man, that ye have no company with him, to the end that he may be ashamed." The authority of the written word of God is

clearly found here. Paul had set forth a pattern that he expected to be followed.

Philippians 4:9, "The things which ye both learned and received and heard and saw in me, these things do: and the God of peace shall be with you." Here again is another clear pattern verse. Paul expected his readers to follow his example and his teachings.

Romans 16:17, "Now I beseech you, brethren, mark them that are causing the divisions and occasions of stumbling, contrary to the doctrine which ye learned, and turn away from them." The pattern is to be followed to the point that those who do not follow it are to be marked and turned away from.

Colossians 4:16, "And when this epistle hath been read among you, cause that it be read also in the church of the Laodiceans; and that ye also read the epistle from Laodecia." Why this instruction? What Paul taught in one church--he taught in every church. In other words, there is a pattern.

The Pattern from 1 Corinthians

The following eight verses show there is a pattern principle in the New Testament after which Christianity is to be ordered.

1 Corinthians 1:10, "Now I beseech you, brethren, through the name of our Lord Jesus Christ, that ye all speak the same thing, and that there be no divisions among you; but that ye be perfected together in the same mind and in the same judgment." Notice the four phrases--speak the same thing, no divisions, same mind,

and same judgment. There is an obvious appeal to follow a prescribed pattern.

1 Corinthians 4:6, "Now these things, brethren, I have in a figure transferred to myself and Apollos for your sakes; that in us ye might learn not to go beyond the things which are written; that no one of you be puffed up for the one against the other." What is written is authoritative. The fact that one is not to go beyond what is written proves there is a pattern, a standard to follow.

1 Corinthians 4:17, "For this cause have I sent unto you Timothy, who is my beloved and faithful child in the Lord, who shall put you in remembrance of my ways which are in Christ, even as I teach everywhere in every church." What Paul taught in one church, he taught in every church. Thus, you have a pattern.

1 Corinthians 7:17, "Only, as the Lord hath distributed to each man, as God hath called each, so let him walk. And so ordain I in all the churches." Notice what Paul ordained in one church, he ordained in every church. Here is a pattern.

1 Corinthians 11:2, "Now, I praise you that ye remember me in all things, and hold fast the traditions, even as I delivered them to you." Please notice they were to "hold the traditions" which were "delivered" unto them. Again, we have a pattern.

1 Corinthians 11:23, "For I received of the Lord that which also I delivered unto you, that the Lord Jesus in the night in which he was betrayed took bread." What Paul "received of the Lord" he "delivered" over to the

Corinthian Christians. These are military terms. This verse is teaching a pattern to be followed.

1 Corinthians 14:33-34, "For God is not a God of confusion, but of peace. As in all the churches of the saints, let the women keep silence in the churches: for it is not permitted unto them to speak; but let them be in subjection as also saith the law." Notice "as in all the churches of the saints" there is a pattern.

1 Corinthians 16:1-2, "Now concerning the collection for the saints, as I gave order to the churches of Galatia, so also do ye. Upon the first day of every week let each one of you lay by him in store, as he may prosper, that no collections be made when I come." What Paul taught to the churches of Galatia, he taught to the church at Corinth. Again, what Paul taught to one church he taught to every church.

These eight passages from 1 Corinthians teach there is an obvious pattern. The word pattern in Greek is *tupos*. *Tupos* is used of a "pattern in conformity to which a thing must be made" (***Thayer's Greek Lexicon***, p. 632), as in Acts 7:44 where God commanded to make the tabernacle. The word is used in Hebrews 8:5, "Even as Moses is warned of God when he is about to make the tabernacle: for See, saith he, that thou make all things according to the pattern (Greek *tupos*) that was showed thee in the mount."

The word "form" in Romans 6:17 has a marginal reading of "pattern" in the ASV 1901. The Greek word translated "form" or "pattern" is *tupos*. Ed Wharton wrote, "A pattern, then, may be thought of as a mold in which lead is poured, and each time the same image is reproduced. Biblically speaking, the pattern concept should produce the idea of distinct doctrinal identity. Consequently, when the New Testament pattern is used for building twentieth century churches, they will identify with those original apostolic churches which conformed to that same doctrinal pattern. The pattern principle thus becomes the restoration principle for first century Christianity" (*The Church of Christ*, p. 5). Amen!

The Charge to Keep the Pattern

2 Thessalonians 2:15, **"Hold the teachings."** This verse is clear. We are to hold to the apostolic teachings. Thus, we are following Jesus (Luke 10:16; John 13:20).

1 Timothy 1:3, "As I exhorted thee to tarry at Ephesus, when I was going into Macedonia, that thou mightest charge certain men not to teach a different doctrine." One doctrine is not as good as another doctrine. This verse teaches that there is a true doctrine whereby one can determine what is false. There must be a doctrinal pattern by which doctrinal differences can be identified. If not, how could Paul carry out this command?

1 Timothy 4:13, "Till I come, give heed to reading, to exhortation, to teaching." The fact that Timothy was to give heed to reading and teaching implies that there is a certain doctrine (i.e. a pattern) to follow.

1 Timothy 6:3-4, "If any man teacheth a different doctrine, and consenteth not to sound words, even the words of our Lord Jesus Christ, and to the doctrine which

is according to godliness; he is puffed up, knowing nothing." The fact that one can teach a "different doctrine" implies that there is a "correct doctrine" (i.e. a pattern) to follow.

Titus 1:10-11, "For there are many unruly men, vain talkers and deceivers, specially they of the circumcision, whose mouths must be stopped; men who overthrow whole houses, teaching things which they ought not, for filthy lucre's sake." Notice the charge to stop the mouths of unruly men and vain talkers. This implies a correct pattern of truth to judge falsehood.

Hebrews 13: 9, "Be not carried away by divers and strange teachings." The fact that it is possible to follow strange teachings implies a standard of truth to evaluate the false teaching.

Jude 3, "Contend earnestly for the faith which was once for all delivered unto the saints." Notice the charge to fight for the faith.

What Is the Pattern?

In simple terms, the pattern is the New Testament. Anything more is too much, and anything less is not enough.

Matthew 4:4, "Man shall not live by bread alone, but by every word that proceedeth out of the mouth of God." Since we are to live by the word of God, it is the pattern.

John 12:48, "He that rejecteth me, and receiveth not my sayings, hath one that judgeth him: the word that I spake, the same shall judge him on the last day." Whatever is going to judge is the pattern to follow.

1 Corinthians 4:6, "That in us ye might learn not to go beyond the things which are written." The written word of God is the pattern and authority.

1 Corinthians 14:37, "If any man thinketh himself to be a prophet, or spiritual, let him take knowledge of the things which I write unto you, that they are the commandment of the Lord." Notice the things that are written by Paul are the commandment of the Lord. What is written is a pattern to follow. To go against Paul is to go against the Lord.

2 Thessalonians 2:15, "So then, brethren, stand fast, and hold the teachings which ye were taught, whether by word (i.e. the oral word), or by epistle (i.e. the written word) of ours." Since we only have today the written word, we are to hold the teachings of the written word. Thus, the written word of the New Testament becomes the pattern to follow.

Hebrews 10:9, "He taketh away the first (i.e. the Old Testament written covenant), that he may establish the second (i.e. the New Testament written covenant)." The second covenant (i.e. the New Testament) is our pattern.

Revelation 20:12, "The dead were judged out of the things which were written in the books (i.e. the books of the Bible)." Since we will judged by the things which were written in the books, these things becomes the pattern to live by.

Conclusion

On page 12 of his book *The Church of Christ*, Ed Wharton wrote, "The systematic study of Scripture reveals the truth that Christianity is ordered after a pattern and that it possesses a distinct identity. Christianity was originally designed by the Lord, preached by the apostles, and practiced by the early church. Christians are commanded to hold the pattern of these sound words. On the basis of this pattern principle, the church of Jesus Christ in its pure apostolic form can be identified and reproduced in the twentieth century. Only the fact of a pattern principle can make the following exhortation a word of practicability: 'O Timothy, guard that which is committed unto thee, turning away from the profane babblings and oppositions of the knowledge which is falsely so called; which some professing have erred concerning the faith' (1 Timothy 6:20-21)."

One note of extremely important concern--we must be aware of the problem of identifying the details of the pattern. Liberals in our brotherhood loose where God has bound and the Legalists (i.e. non-Institutionals) bind where God has loosed. Both of these viewpoints are wrong and sinful. **It will be the job of every generation to continue to study Scripture to determine what is bound by God and what is open for human liberty to choose.**

For Thought or Discussion

1. What happened to Weldon Bennett? Where was the problem?
2. When Paul said "Hold the pattern" what does this imply?
3. (True or False) Christians are to "hold the teachings" based on the New Testament written word.
4. What is the Greek word translated "form" or "pattern" in Romans 6:17? Define it.
5. How is Philippians 4:9 a pattern principle verse?
6. What does the fact that one is not to go beyond what is written prove?
7. (True or False) What Paul taught in one church, he taught in every church.
8. What Scriptures teach that Jesus endorsed the writings of Paul as authoritative for Christians today? (Give at least three.)
9. What does 1 Timothy 1:3 imply?
10. What is the very important problem in identifying the details of the pattern?
11. What will judge us on the last day?
12. (True or False) The pattern principle of the New Testament becomes the restoration principle of first century Christianity.
13. What is the job of every generation?
14. What do 2 Timothy 1:13 and 2 Thessalonians 2:15 clearly teach?
15. What is the difference between liberalism and legalism?

6

Acceptable Worship to God

The word "worship" is defined "reverence or devotion for a deity; religious homage or veneration; a church service or other rite showing this; extreme devotion or intense love or admiration of any kind."

Today in Churches of Christ, many brethren are seeking to implement changes into the worship service on the grounds that it is appealing, invigorating, motivating, and uplifting. Liberal brethren want the piano, solos, choirs, entertainment, praise teams and the like to be used in the worship service. They say we are dying numerically and if we do not change, we will die. Soren Kierkegaard said, "Passionate worship of an idol is better than a cold, formal worship of God." In other words, excitement with error overrules righteousness and truth. He was dead wrong. Worship is to be according to "truth" (John 4:24)--not feelings or subjective opinions. Without "truth" all worship becomes self-willed worship and is condemned according to Scripture (Col. 3:17, 23). Excitement with error does not overrule righteousness and truth. **If our worship is not according to truth, God does not accept it (John 4:23-24).**

Righteousness is more important to God than growth. Consider the flood--only 8 souls were saved. Consider Sodom and Gomorrah--less than 10 were saved. Consider Judgment Day--only a "few" (Matt. 7:13-14) will be saved. On the Day of Judgment many sincere people will be surprised that are eternally lost (Matt. 7:21-23). Regardless of what some think, today in modern America we can preach the gospel and do the fundamentals well and grow. My wife and I have helped 5 churches grow (89 to 185; 48 to 156; 41 to 85; 65 to 100; 56 to 114). Presently, we are working with a church that is also growing. Therefore, do not tell me you have to change and implement excitement and change into the worship service to grow. It is absolutely not true! Gary Hill wrote, "All surveys point to the fact that what people want are churches that stand for something! The watered down theology of so many churches lead the members to conclude that they can get just as much from 'worshipping' at the country club, golf course or fishing hole as they're likely to get at their local church service."

The extremely important point is that we must **not** worship according to what "we think" would be appropriate. We must worship according to what God thinks! God Himself said, "For my thought are not your thoughts, neither are your ways my ways" (Isa. 55:8). It is absolutely essential to read and study the Bible to discover the nature of acceptable worship!

Read Genesis 4:1-7 and Hebrews 11:4

Notice that both Cain and Abel made an "offering unto Jehovah." Jehovah had "respect" for Abel's offering but for Cain's God had "not respect." John said that Cain's "works were evil, and his brother's righteous" (1 John 3:12). The word "evil" here means "sinful and disobedient." The Hebrew writer said "Abel offered unto God a more excellent sacrifice than Cain, through which he had witness borne to him that he was righteous, God bearing witness in respect of his gifts: and through it **he being dead yet speaketh** (Heb. 11:4). Abel was "righteous" because he obeyed God. Righteousness is right doing. It is keeping the commandments (Psa. 119:172). Even though Abel is dead, his actions still speak to us today. If we want to be righteous, we must be obedient to God and give God what He requires--not what we want to give Him! John wrote, "He that doeth righteousness is righteous" (1 John 3:7).

Read Genesis 22:1-5

Do you know where the word "worship" is first found in Scripture? It is Genesis 22:5 where Abraham says, "I and the lad will go yonder; and we will worship." This defines what worship involves. The best definition is a biblical definition. I want to ask a simple but direct question! Was Abraham doing what he wanted to do or what God wanted Abraham to do? The answer is Abraham was obeying God! Abraham did not want to kill his beloved son Isaac. He did not feel good about it. He was not in the mood to do it. But, the bottom line was he was going to be obedient to God. **That is the fundamental concept of worship--obedience to God. Worship is not doing what we want or what is appealing to us--it is obedience to God.**

Read Leviticus 10:1-4

Notice that Nadab and Abihu "offered strange fire before Jehovah, which he had not commanded them." The word "strange" is defined by ***Brown-Driver-Briggs Hebrew Lexicon*** as "unlawful." ***Owens Hebrew***

Lexicon defines it as "unholy." The fire that they offered was "unlawful." It was not according to what God had commanded them. As a result, "There came forth fire from before Jehovah, and devoured them, and they died before Jehovah." Nadab and Abihu offered their own method of worship to God. It was self-willed not God-willed. When we approach God in worship, we better take it seriously. We must worship according to the plan He has set forth for us. Worship is not what we want to give to Him. Notice verse 3. God says, "I will be sanctified in them that come nigh me." In other words God is teaching--My plan of worship must be accepted and followed.

Read 1 Samuel 13:1-14

Saul was not a priest and therefore was not allowed to offer a sacrifice in worship to Jehovah. Verse 8 states, "And he tarried seven days, according to the set time that Samuel had appointed: but Samuel came not to Gilgal." Saul was to wait for Samuel. On the 7th day Samuel had not arrived. So, Saul took it upon himself to offer the sacrifice. In verse 9, we read Saul "offered the burnt offering." He was supposed to wait for Samuel. He sinned. On the 7th day immediately after Saul had offered the sacrifice, Samuel came as promised. Notice Saul's reasoning. First, the people were scattered. Second, Samuel had not yet come. Third, the Philistines were assembled for battle. Fourth, he wanted God's favor. But, all that reasoning was in vain. Did any one, just one, of those reasons justify Saul offering the sacrifice? Absolutely not! The bottom line was Saul disobeyed God! Remember Isaiah 55:8 where God says, "For my thoughts are not your thoughts, neither are your ways my ways." Notice 1 Samuel 13:13 says, "And Samuel said to Saul, Thou hast done foolishly; thou hast not kept the commandment of Jehovah thy God, which he commanded thee." Sin is doing foolishly! The result was that Jehovah took Saul's kingdom away from him (1 Sam. 13:14). Sin always has a price and consequence to pay and it is never a pleasant experience. When it comes to worshipping God, we must worship according to His plan--not what we want or what we think!

Read 1 Samuel 15:1-35

In verse 3, Saul is told, "Now go and smite Amalek, and utterly destroy all that they have, and spare them not; but slay both man and woman, infant and suckling, ox and sheep, camel and ass." But, Saul disobeyed God. In verse 8, we read that Saul "took Agag the king of the Amalekites alive." In verse 9, we find that Saul "spared Agag, and the best of the sheep, and of the oxen, and of the fatlings, and the lambs, and all that was good, and would not utterly destroy them." In verse 19, Samuel said, "Wherefore then didst thou not obey the voice of Jehovah, but didst fly upon the spoil, and didst that which was evil in the sight of Jehovah?" Notice that sin is defined as "evil." (In the Old Testament the word "evil" has three meanings--sin, chastisement, or calamity. The context must determine its meaning.) In verse 21, Saul tried blaming the sparing of the animals on the people and that the animals were going to be used in sacrifice to Jehovah. **Then in verse 22, we have a classic Bible verse: "Behold, to obey is better than sacrifice." In other words, it is more important to be obedient to God and give God what He requires than for man to give God what man wants to give!** This is the fundamental principle behind worshipping God. It does not matter what we want--what matters is what God wants! Saul's act of disobedience was "rebellion" (verse 23). Samuel told Saul, "Because thou hast rejected the word of Jehovah, he hath also rejected thee from being king" (verse 23). I wish our brethren would learn this very important principle. When it comes to the worship service--are we doing what God wants or what we want to do?

2 Samuel 6:6-7

"And they came to the threshing-floor of Nacon, Uzzah put forth his hand to the ark of God, and took hold of it; for the oxen stumbled. And the anger of Jehovah was kindled against Uzzah; and God smote him there for his error; and there he died by the ark of God."

One might wonder why God killed Uzzah on the spot. The oxen stumbled and Uzzah was simply trying to stop the ark from falling. One might say he was trying to help God. But, Numbers 4:15 gave a clear warning. Numbers 4:15 states, "They shall not touch the sanctuary (i.e. the Ark of the Covenant), lest they die." God had warned the priests do not touch the Ark of the Covenant because if you do, you will die. The bottom line was Uzzah disobeyed God. His act was called "error" ASV 1901. The marginal reading has "rashness." The NKJV has "irreverence" in the margin. Uzzah's act was irreverent because he disobeyed a clear declaration of Jehovah. In Exodus 25:10-22 God had given instructions on how to transport the Ark of the Covenant. The ark had rings on it and poles were to be used to carry it so that no one touched it. However, they were carrying the ark on a "new cart" (2 Sam. 6:3) and not with the poles as God had directed. One sin led to another sin! From this story we learn that God demands obedience. We must give God what He wants--not what we want to give to Him.

Matthew 15: 8-9

"This people honoreth me with their lips; But their heart is far from me. But in vain do they worship me, teaching as their doctrines the precepts of men."

In this passage, Jesus rebukes the Pharisees for **"vain"** worship. "Vain" worship is "empty, useless, worthless, hollow, having no real value or significance, unprofitable, unavailing." The Pharisees were seeking ways out of supporting their parents. The Fifth of the Ten Commandments was: "Honor thy Father and thy Mother" (Exodus 20:12). The word "honor" meant more than just to give respect. It also meant to take care them of when they got old. The Pharisees thought they had found a way around the Fifth Commandment. Jesus rebukes them and says, "And ye have made void the word of God because of your tradition" (Matt. 15:6). The lesson for us is if we try to bypass the clear teaching of God's word, our worship is "vain."

John 4:23-24

"But the hour cometh, and now is, when the true worshippers shall worship the Father in spirit and truth: for such doth the Father seek to be his worshippers. God is spirit: and they

that worship him must worship in spirit and truth."

Granville Sharp's rule of Greek grammar says when one preposition precedes two nouns connected by the word "and," the two nouns are to be taken together as a unit. (This is exactly what we have in John 4:24 and also in John 3:5--"of water and spirit.") Acceptable worship to God must be given **"in spirit and truth."** There are two conditions and each is just as important as the other. To minimize one and exalt one over the other is wrong. "In spirit" refers to the right purpose, right attitude, right intent, with sincerity. "Truth" refers to the word of God, right act, right mode. For example, take the Lord's Supper. "Spirit" refers to how one partakes. One must partake thinking of Christ's death. Jesus said, "This do in remembrance of me" (1 Cor. 11:24). We should not be thinking about our job, our week, or anything else. "Truth" refers to the right act, the right mode. We are to use unleavened bread and fruit of the vine. These elements are very easy to obtain. One liberal brother in Lawn, Texas thought that one could use Fritos and Coca-Cola in the Lord's Supper. I am not kidding. Take baptism for another example. The purpose of baptism is "unto the remission of sins" (Acts 2:38); "wash away sins" (Acts 22:16); for salvation (Mark 16:16; 1 Pet. 3:21); to come into Christ where salvation is (Rom. 6:3-4; Eph. 1:3; 2 Tim. 2:10). It is not because one's sins have already been forgiven. It is not an outward sign of an inward grace. The mode of baptism is immersion. The Greek word *rhantizo* means sprinkling. The Greek word *cheo* means pour. One who has been sprinkled on or poured on has not been baptized!

Read Romans 10:1-3

These verses teach that sincerity alone does not equal approval from God. Many people think as long as they are sincere, they are acceptable with God. This text teaches the error of that interpretation. Dwight Robarts, a liberal preacher in our brotherhood, said, "Every group of people who sincerely seeks to be what God has called them to be in the world is the church that belongs to Christ." This is heresy of the highest order! **Sincerity by itself does not mean we are accepted with God**. Paul said that "beyond measure I persecuted the church of God and made havoc of it" (Gal. 1:13). Acts 8:3 states, "But Saul laid waste the church, entering into every house, and dragging men and women committed them to prison." Paul said, "I have lived in all good conscience until this day" (Acts 23:1). He also said, "I verily thought with myself that I ought to do many things contrary to the name of Jesus of Nazareth" (Acts 26:9). **Paul was sincere, but he was sincerely wrong.** Proverbs 14:12 states, "There is a way which seemeth right unto a man; But the end thereof are the ways of death." When one is ignorant of the truth, his worship cannot be acceptable to God. This is why we must always go back and study the Bible and find the truth that God wants us to follow.

Read Colossians 2:20-23

Paul uses the word "will-worship" in Colossians 2:23 to designate worship unacceptable to God. The expression "will-worship" is from the single Greek word *ethelothreskeia*. Thayer defines this word as meaning "arbitrary worship." J. B. Rotherham and Benjamin Wilson translate it as "self-devised worship." The NASV translates it "self-made religion." The NKJV translates it as "self-imposed religion." Any form of worship not authorized by God's word, but originating with man, is certainly arbitrary and self-devised. Before seeking changing any form of the worship service, we need to ask, "Is this approved of by God Almighty?" Lenski says it is "a self-chosen worship that is willed by the will of those who want it and not a type of worship that is willed by God." Thayer depicted will-worship as: "worship which one devises and prescribes for himself, contrary to the contents and nature of the faith which ought to be directed to Christ." Will-worship is arrogant and autocratic. It reflects the self-inflated attitude of Jeroboam who devised a worship format "of his own heart" through which he "made Israel to sin" (1 Kings 14:16). Sadly, unfortunately, in the Lord's Church an absurd variety of changes have been proposed to accommodate modern will-worship. We should all heed the advice of Proverbs 14:12 which says, "There is a way which seemeth right unto a man; but the end thereof is the way of death."

Colossians 3:17

"And whatsoever ye do, in word or in deed, do all in the name of the Lord Jesus, giving thanks to God the Father through him."

The expression "in the name of" means "by the authority of." When I send a student with a pass and my signature is on the pass, my name gives the student the authority to go do what I have sent him to do. Whatever we do in religion we must have authority for. When brethren want to put in praise teams, women waiting on the table, women leading prayers at the table, they need to stop and ask--where is the authority for this. If there is no authority, then it is sinful to do it.

Conclusion

When we approach God in worship, our attitude must not be--this is what I want or this is what feels good to me or this is what is invigorating to me. Our attitude must be--what does God want or is this pleasing to God? The apostle John wrote, "Beloved, believe not every spirit, but prove the spirits, whether they are of God; because many false prophets are gone out into the world" (1 John 4:1). Just because someone is sincere, that does not make him right (Rom. 10:1-3)! Just because someone quotes the Bible, that does not make him right (2 Pet. 3:15-17). Satan quoted Scripture, but he distorted the meaning (Matt. 4:5-7). The Pharisees could quote Scripture (John 8:5) but many times they were in error (Matt. 23:1-33). Even Hitler could quote Scripture. We must examine every preacher with the word of God.

For Thought or Discussion

1. Define the word "worship." (use Genesis 22:5)
2. The liberals think we need to implement changes to grow. Are they justified? Why?
3. What can we learn from the story about Nadab and Abihu? (Lev. 10:1-3)
4. (True or False) Sin is foolishness.
5. Explain: "To obey is better than sacrifice" (1 Sam. 15:22).
6. (True or False) It is okay to disobey God if you are trying to help God.
7. What are some other meanings to the word "error" in 2 Samuel 6:7?
8. (True or False) Sincerity in worship is more important than the act.
9. Discuss John 4:23-24.
10. What are the 3 meanings of the word "evil" in the Old Testament?
11. What does "will-worship" mean? (Col. 2:20-23)
12. Define the expression--"in the name of" in Colossians 3:17.
13. How were the Pharisees guilty of "vain" religion in Matthew 15: 1-9?
14. (True or False) One's conscience determines truth.
15. What does 1 John 4:1 teach?
16. (True or False) Quoting the Bible indicates the person has truth on his side.
17. (True or False) Liberals are right when they say we have to change to grow.
18. What is the force of Isaiah 55:8?

7

Instrumental Music? #1

When non-members of the Church of Christ walk in most of our buildings, the first thing they notice is that we do not have a piano. The reason is not because we cannot afford them. The reason is there is no authority to have them. We are not trying to be high and mighty, proud, or arrogant. We simply have a deep and abiding desire to follow the commands of God in His word! Some people say it is a petty thing whether you use a piano or not. We strongly disagree! No question about worshipping God is a petty thing. Ask Nadab and Abihu.

Jehovah Is the Holy God

We must understand that Jehovah is the holy God. God said, "Ye shall be holy; for I Jehovah your God am holy" (Lev. 19:2). Peter wrote, "But like as he who called you is holy, be ye yourselves also holy in all manner of living; because it written, Ye shall be holy; for I am holy" (1 Pet. 1:15-16). Isaiah 6:3 states, "Holy, holy, holy, is Jehovah of hosts." Revelation 4:8 states, "Holy, holy, holy, is the Lord God, the Almighty." The word "holy" means "set apart, belonging to or coming from God, consecrated, sacred, untainted by evil or sin; regarded with or deserving deep respect, awe, reverence, or adoration." God says, "I hate every false way" (Psa. 119:104). We must come to understand the importance of holiness. Hebrews 12:14 (KJV) states, "Without holiness no man shall see the Lord." If we are not living a holy life, we will not enter heaven!

When it comes to the question, should we have a piano or organ in the worship service, the question should be: What does God say about it? We should not use a piano because it appeals to us, or because we like it, or because visitors would like it. Paul said, "Proving what is well-pleasing unto the Lord" (Eph. 5:10). He also said, "Prove all things; hold fast that which is good" (1 Thess. 5:21). Only that which we can prove acceptable is good! Can instrumental music in worship be defended? We believe the answer is a resounding no!

The Battle before Us

The year 1906 is given as the time of the official split between Churches of Christ and The Christian Church. (The Churches of Christ refused to use the instrument while the Christian Church favored its use.) However, from 1846 to 1906 Churches of Christ all over America were splitting because of the instrument. I preached at Cold Springs Church of Christ in Lancaster, Texas from 1982 to 1996. That Church split in 1846 over the instrument. In 1932, the Christian Church split into The Christian Church and the Disciples of Christ. The Disciples of Christ are the far left-wing body of the Restoration Movement. Sadly, unfortunately, over the last 20-40 years there are some Churches of Christ which have started using the instrument in their worship services. Some say it is a congregational issue that each congregation decides for itself. We totally disagree with that assessment. In 1995, in a *Dallas Morning News* article of June 3, Steven Polk, the Minister of Music at

Farmers Branch Church of Christ, said, "The banning of musical instruments is more of a tradition than something based on Scripture." Brethren, that is definitely not true! It is because of Scripture that we are vehemently opposed to using musical instruments in worship! Polk does not know his Bible or history!

In September 1999, the eldership of the Oak Hills Church of Christ in San Antonio (where Max Lucado preached) gave this written announcement in their bulletin, "The elders want to provide you with a question that many have raised. That question has to do with the use of musical instruments in our worship. After many months of careful study and consideration, the elders unanimously concluded that there is no Biblical prohibition of the use of musical instruments in worship." The fact that an eldership or college or religious editor or any group votes to determine truth should not impress us. Truth is not determined by a majority vote or by some group of elders! Spiritual truth is determined by the word of God (John 17:17). Can you imagine a math class where the correct answer is determined by a majority vote of the students? Ludicrous! Truth is determined by the facts--not a vote! Where did the apostasy start anyway? It was in the elders (Acts 20:17-32). An eldership in Tennessee voted 8 to 3 that musical instruments in worship were acceptable.

Howard Norton, executive director of the Institute for Church and Family, Harding University, wrote, "My heart is broken because of the unscriptural changes that are taking place in a small number of Churches of Christ. The introduction of instrumental music into the public assemblies is but

one example. Such changes are neither casual nor cosmetic. They are based on a fundamental shift in attitude toward the New Testament as the authoritative divine guide for the church today. Those making these changes have decided to introduce instrumental music even though there is not a shred of justification for it in the New Testament or in early church history. These people then tell us that they have made no significant change in the church's core values. What a falsehood!" Amen! Conservative brethren agree 100% with Brother Norton.

One of their main arguments for the use of instrumental music is relevancy. Those churches who have started using the instrument say it increases attendance. Keith Luttrell says, "Relevance is driving it. Relevance to our community. Reaching out to seekers." But, I would ask you to re-read the chapter on Worship. What is the main goal for the church? Numbers or Righteousness? These wayward, ignorant brethren who vote to use the instrument have lost the truth on what it takes to worship God! **John Ellas, director of the Center for Church Growth in Houston, Texas, writes, "Others who would like to blame evangelism, relevancy and meeting needs as the culprit for the introduction of instruments miss the real theological shift that has taken place."** Amen! Again, Brother Ellas hits the nail on the head. He is "spot-on."

Today, faithful Christians have a spiritual battle before us. One battle we are facing again is the use of musical instruments in worship. Now is the time to stand against this ungodliness. We must be like Joshua of old: "But as for me and my house, we will serve the LORD"

(Joshua 24:15). Paul said he had "fought the good fight" (2 Tim. 4:7). Jude 3 says, "Contend earnestly for the faith." Are we going to fight the good fight?

The Argument from Early Church History

The Italian word "*a cappella*" means "in the manner of the church" or "as it was in the church" or "as the church does it." The words "*a cappella*" today means "without instrumental accompaniment." This is historical proof of what the early church did in worship. The history of the church conclusively shows that instrumental music was an innovation. For many years no church used instruments in worship. The use of the instrument is of human origin and not of Divine instruction.

In *McClintock and Strong's Cyclopedia* we read, "The general introduction of instrumental music can certainly not be assigned to a date earlier than the fifth or sixth centuries; yea, even Gregory the Great, who towards the end of the sixth century added greatly to the existing Church music, absolutely prohibited the use of instruments" (Vol. V, p.759). Emil Nauman wrote, "There can be no doubt that originally the music of the divine service was everywhere entirely of vocal nature" (*The History of Music*, Vol. I, p.177). *Fessenden's Encyclopedia* says, "Instrumental music was not practiced by the primitive Christians" (p. 852). The *Schaff-Herzog Encyclopedia* states, "In the Greek Church the organ never came into use. But after the eighth century it became more and more common in the Latin Church; not, however, without opposition from the side of the monks" (Vol. II, p. 1702). Hugo Leichtentritt wrote, "Only singing, however, and no playing of instruments, was permitted in the early Christian church" (*Music, History, and Ideas*, p. 34). Lyman Coleman wrote, "It is generally admitted that primitive Christians employed no instrumental music in their religious worship" (*The Primitive Church*, p. 276-277). James W. McKinnon, in his 1965 doctoral dissertation at Columbia University--*The Church Fathers and Musical Instruments*, wrote, "That the early church music was wholly vocal, and that the opposition of the church fathers to instrumental music in worship was both monolithic and vehement." Everett Ferguson wrote the book *A Cappella Music in the Public Worship of the Church*. This church historian cites passages from Ignatius of Antioch, Justin Martyr, Clement of Alexandria, Tertullian, Eusebius, Ambrose, and others, to the effect that the singing of the church of the first several centuries was *a cappella*. James William McKinnon wrote, "The fathers of the early church were virtually unanimous in their hostility against musical instruments." He also said, "There is no reference to Instrumental Music in early church worship in the New Testament, or in the worship of the first six centuries" (*Music in Early Church Literature*, p. 263-265).

The year 1054 A.D. is significant. This year the Greek Orthodox Church split with the Roman Catholic Church. There were a number of reasons, but two of them dealt directly with the misuse of the Greek language. The Greeks knew that *baptizo* meant immersion and that *psallo* meant to sing, nothing more. The Greek Orthodox Church has never permitted instruments in their worship services. If the Greek word "*psallo*" meant to use the instrument, don't you think the Greeks knew it? The word *psallo* is a Greek word!

Denominational Scholars and Instrumental Music

John Wesley (Methodist) said, "I have no objection to the instrument being in our chapels, provided they are neither seen nor heard." Adam Clarke (Methodist) wrote, "Music is a science I esteem and admire, but instrumental music in the house of God I abominate and abhor." Charles Spurgeon (Baptist) wrote, "We do not need them; they would hinder rather than help the praise. We might as well pray by machinery as to praise by it" (***Instrumental Music***, p. 176). Spurgeon never allowed any instruments of music to be used in any of his services. John Calvin (Presbyterian) said, "Musical instruments in celebrating the praises of God would be no more suitable than the burning of incense, the lighting of lamps, and the restoration of the other shadows of the laws." Martin Luther (Lutherans) said, "The organ in the worship to God is an ensign of Baal."

Restoration Leaders and Instrumental Music

The leaders of the Restoration Movement vigorously opposed the use of instruments in worship-- not because of "tradition" but because of a deep respect for Scripture. Alexander Campbell said musical instruments in worship "would be as a cow bell in a concert." Moses Lard said, "What defense can be urged for the introduction into some of our congregations of instrumental music? The answer which thunders into my ear from every page of the New Testament is none. Did

Christ ever appoint it? Did the apostles ever sanction it? Or did any one of the primitive churches ever use it? Never. In what light then must we view him who attempts to introduce it into the Churches of Christ of the present day? I answer, as an insulter of the authority of Christ, and as a defiant and impious innovator in the simplicity and purity of the ancient worship." J. W. McGarvey wrote, "In the earlier years of the present Reformation, there was entire unanimity in the rejection of instrumental music from our public worship. It was declared unscriptural, inharmonious with the Christian institution, and a source of corruption." Other leaders in the Restoration Movement were vehemently opposed to the use of instruments in worship. Men like David Lipscomb, Robert Milligan, M.C. Kurfees, N. B. Hardeman, G. C. Brewer, Foy E. Wallace Jr., and many others were always opposed to the use of the instrument on scriptural grounds--not tradition. Our erring and ignorant brother Steven Polk is dead wrong on his view that we have not used the instrument because of "tradition." He needs a good course in Restoration History, something in which he is woefully lacking. He also needs to understand the correct biblical hermeneutic which will be discussed in the next sub-point!

Musical Instruments: The Problem or Symptom of the Problem?

When a sick person goes to the doctor, it is important to treat the real problem and not the symptoms of the problem. If a person has a malignant tumor, telling him merely to go to bed and get some rest will not solve the real problem. The use of the instrument in worship is only the symptom of the real problem. The real problem is the approach and attitude one takes in understanding Scripture. The issue can be divided into two distinct questions. Can we do anything and everything not specifically and directly condemned? Or, must we do only that which the Bible authorizes? (Bible verses Matt. 4:4; 1 Cor. 4:6; 1 Cor. 14:37; Col. 3:17; and 1 Pet. 4:11 totally support the second question. Acts 15:24 teaches silence does not give permission.) The answer we give to these questions involves the basic difference between the Church of Christ and the rest of the religious world. This is the real issue that must be dealt with before one discusses the instrument.

John L. Giradeau, a Presbyterian scholar at Columbia Theological Seminary, wrote, "The principle of the discretionary power of the church in regard to things not commanded by Christ in His word, was the chief fountain from which flowed the gradually increasing corruption that swept the Latin Church into apostasy from the gospel of God's grace . .. any Protestant church that embodies that principle in its creed is destined sooner or later, to experience a similar fate." What is he saying? When you follow the principle that anything not forbidden in Scripture is okay, you go into apostasy, the church will be corrupted. The apostle Paul said, "And whatsoever ye do, in word or deed, do all in the name of our Lord Jesus, giving thanks to God the Father through him" (Col. 3:17). Whatever we do to worship God, we must have authority. At the start of the Protestant Reformation, Martin Luther held the view that whatever was not specifically forbidden in Scripture might be employed in Christian worship. Zwingli devoutly believed in the absolute authority of

Scripture. He held that whatever was not expressly authorized was forbidden in worship. There were others that sided with Zwingli. This is the battleground today. Are we going to open the floodgates to what is not prohibited? If so, we are opening Pandora's Box. The Bible does not say we cannot add peanut butter and jelly to the Lord's Supper. Some would even argue that more would come to services if we did add peanut butter and jelly to the Lord's Supper. But, is something right just because it is not expressly forbidden? No! Why? Because we live by what God says not by what He did not say.

Many religious people scoff, ridicule, and laugh at us for even thinking that instrumental music in worship might possibly be a sin. These people are ignorant of biblical teaching. Their hermeneutical principles are wrong. The Hebrew writer said, "It is a fearful thing to fall into the hands of the living God" (Heb. 10:31) and "For our God is a consuming fire" (Heb. 12:29). Paul said, "Knowing therefore the fear of the Lord, we persuade men" (2 Cor. 5:11). We need to have some fear and reverential respect for God's commands. They must not be taken lightly. Instrumental music is definitely not a "petty" thing.

Singing Is a Specific Command

In Mark 16:15 Jesus said, "Go ye into all the world, and preach the gospel to the whole creation." The command "go" is a generic command. "How" we go is left up to us. In 1 Timothy 5:16 the Church is commanded to take care of widows that cannot take care of themselves. "How" we do this is left up to us. If we try to bind where God has given freedom, we become "forbidding" brethren and are guilty of sin (1 Tim. 4:1-5). However, singing is a specific command, a specific type of music. If God had said just "make music," then we would be free to use any or all of the three types of music (vocal, instrumental, or vocal and instrumental combined). But, God gave us the specific command to sing. That specific command automatically excludes any other kind.

There are ten passages in the New Testament that specifically refer to sing or singing: Matthew 26:29; Mark 14:26; Acts 16:25; Romans 15:9; 1 Corinthians 14:15; Ephesians 5:19; Colossians 3:16; Hebrews 2:12; Hebrews 13:15; James 5:13. When God gives specific commands, we must obey exactly as God says. If we add to a specific command, we sin! Adam and Eve had a specific command, and they violated it and were punished. Noah had a specific command to make the ark out of gopher wood. It would have been wrong for Noah to use anything other than gopher wood. Nadab and Abihu had a specific command on what fire to use in worship. They violated that command and were devoured by fire from heaven. Moses had a specific command to speak to the rock but he struck the rock and was not allowed to enter the Promised Land (Numbers 20: 7-13). Uzzah had a specific command not to touch the ark (Num. 4:15). He violated that command and lost his life. Naaman had a specific command to dip in the river Jordan seven times. He had to go specifically to the river Jordan and no other. He had to dip seven times--not three or five. The man born blind in John 9 had a specific command. He had to go to the Pool of Siloam and wash. The specific Pool of Siloam meant that he could not go to any other pool. When God Almighty gives us a specific command, we must obey the specific command.

Conclusion

It is not because of "tradition" that we do not use the instrument. When we refuse to use mechanical instruments in worship, we show a deep and abiding respect for the word of God. We have two clear choices. We can do only that which is authorized by the word of God. Or, we can do anything not expressly condemned in Scripture. But, if we do that we open the flood gates. The Bible does not say I cannot have 10 wives. It does not say I cannot add steak and potatoes to the Lord's Supper. The Bible does not say I cannot substitute Fritos and Coca-Cola for unleavened bread and fruit of the vine. And on and on we could go!

Nadab and Abihu were sons of the high priest, Aaron (the brother of Moses). They offered a "strange fire" unto the Lord. The word "strange" in Hebrew means "unlawful." This is an example and warning to us as Christians (Rom. 15:4; 1 Cor. 10:1-11). We cannot change what God has said regarding our worship. Instrumental music is a "strange fire" in the sight of God Almighty.

For Thought or Discussion

1. What are the implications of Hebrews 12:14?
2. How is truth determined? (John 17:17)
3. If an eldership makes a decision that contradicts the word of God, what should we do? (2 Tim. 4:1-5)
4. What did Howard Norton say about Churches of Christ that have changed and use the instrument in worship?
5. (True or False) The goal of having more numbers proves Instrumental Music is acceptable to God.
6. Which is more important to God--righteousness or numbers?
7. Define the Italian phrase *a cappella*. What does this imply?
8. What do church historians say about the music of the first century Church?
9. Discuss the significance of the year 1054 A.D.
10. What did Denominational scholars and Restoration leaders say about Instrumental Music?
11. (True or False) Instrumental music is the symptom of the real problem.
12. What is the real problem behind Instrumental Music?
13. What did John Giradeau say about how we go into apostasy? Do you agree? Why?
14. What is the significance of a specific command?
15. (True or False) Churches of Christ have rejected Instrumental Music because of "tradition."
16. What did John Ellas say about the use of Instrumental Music in worship?

17. (True or False) It is acceptable to God to substitute Fritos and Coca-Cola for unleavened bread and fruit of the vine in the Lord's Supper. Why?

18. (True or False) Any Christian has the right to reprove any elder who teaches false doctrine. (cf. 2 Tim. 4:1-5; Acts 20:17-32)

8

Instrumental Music? #2

The Law of Inclusion and Exclusion

This point is very similar to the point that singing is a specific command. Every one of us lives by this law every day. Suppose you go to McDonalds and you order a Big Mac and a Coke. Let us suppose that the attendant adds an apple pie and starts to charge you for the apple pie. You respond, "Wait just a minute. I did not order the apple pie so you cannot charge me for it." Certainly, you are correct. Every person recognizes this rule. When you place an order for specific items, that order automatically excludes other items. When I give a test and I tell my students do the even numbered problems, that command automatically excludes the odd numbered problems. When God specifically tells us what to do, that automatically excludes anything else. We live by what God says—not by what God does not say (Matt. 4:4; 1 Cor. 4:6; 1 Cor. 14:37; Col. 3:17; 2 Thess. 2:15). When God specifically says sing, that command rules out instrumental or a combination of vocal and instrumental. But brethren, please, please, please be aware of this important fact: There is a big, big difference between an "aid" and an "addition" to follow a command.

God commanded Noah to build an ark 300 cubits long and build it out of gopher wood. The permissible aids to obey God's command were tools to cut, join, and to spread pitch. Sinful additions would be a larger or smaller size, additional windows, or a different type of wood than gopher wood.

God told Moses to build the ark of the covenant out of acacia wood and make it two and a half cubits long (Numbers 25:10). The permissible aids would be the tools to build it. Sinful additions would be making it out of acacia wood plus some other type of wood or not making it out of acacia wood. Also, changing the size would be an unlawful addition.

When it comes to the Lord's Supper, we are to use unleavened bread and fruit of the vine. Permissible aids would be trays and cups. Note: some brethren say we must use only one cup. But, when Jesus said drink the cup, he meant to drink the contents of the cup--not the cup itself. It is impossible to literally drink the cup. That is absurd. Some brethren bind where God has loosed. Sinful additions would be to add meat and potatoes. It would also be sinful to substitute Fritos and Coca-Cola for the unleavened bread and fruit of the vine.

When it comes to baptism, it must be by immersion. Permissible aids would be a baptistery, pool, river, lake, sea, or bathtub. Sinful changes would be to sprinkle or pour and call that baptism. (The Greek word *baptizo* means immersion. The Greek word *rhantizo* means sprinkle. The Greek word *cheo* mean pour.)

When God says sing, that command is vocal music only. The Law of Inclusion and Exclusion rules out any additions. Permissible aids would be a songbook or pitch pipe. It is impossible to start a song without pitch. A pitch pipe is used to obtain the correct pitch for that song. Sinful additions would be a piano or organ or guitar, etc.

Words from a Minister of Music in the Christian Church

Tom Lawson is a minister of music for an independent Christian Church, a body which uses instrumental music. He wrote an article pointing out three advantages of *a cappella* worship. We need to listen to this man.

First, "It tends to maintain the central players in worship as a congregation rather than the performers up front. When the music of worship is the music of the church itself, it seems less likely that we will move from worship to watching worship. The worth of a particular service is, many times, gauged by the quality of the performances. Applause is not merely tolerated, it is expected."

Second, "It tends to preserve times of silence within corporate worship. My church feels obligated to not allow a single moment of silence within the entire worship experience. Every moment when someone is not speaking or singing must be filled with the organ or piano. I do not need my moods programmed at every moment."

Third, "It tends to preserve a simplicity of worship that may be increasingly attractive in our complicated age. I am baffled why some within the Church of Christ would pick this time to move toward inclusion of the instrument in worship. Doesn't the growing attraction of everything from *a cappella* secular music to Gregorian chants give indication that less may be more and that simplicity and times of silence may have an attraction as great as the big performance?"

After these three points, Tom wrote, "To my friends within the Church of Christ, I would encourage you to think long and hard before you join the rest of the evangelical world in this area that so clearly impacts the entire worship service. I find myself wishing that, at least once in a while, we'd close up the piano, turn off the organ, unplug the guitars and just see what would happen."

Some of our brotherhood leaders need to take heed to what Tom has said. As far as I am concerned, Tom's article speaks volumes. Admittedly, Tom did not approach Instrumental Music from a scriptural standpoint. He only approached it from a view of improving the worship service. What does this say to those elders and preachers that instrumental music is needed to improve the service? It says that instrumental music is not needed to improve the service. Several years ago a Baptist lady told me that she went to a funeral at a Church of Christ and was very impressed with the congregational singing. She loved it and thought it was wonderful. It is very interesting that she belonged to a church that used the instrument but was overwhelmed with the beauty of congregational singing! I have received similar comments like this many times in my life.

A Simple Question and a Simple Appeal

We know that using only vocal music in the worship service is acceptable to God Almighty. Even those who favor using the instrument acknowledge that using only vocal music is acceptable. **A simple question is why move from a position that you know is right to a position that is highly debated and controversial and called sin by many faithful brethren?**

The story is told of a very wealthy man who needed to hire a chauffeur. Three men applied for the job. One of the difficult parts of the test was driving around a cliff. The first driver came within one foot of the cliff. The second driver thought he needed to do better than that. So, he drove within six inches of the cliff. He thought he had the job won and the third driver could not do better. When the third driver drove around the cliff, he stayed as far away from the cliff as possible. Guess who got the job? The third driver! Why? The wealthy man did not want his driver taking chances when he did not have to take chances. I wish that our liberal brethren who favor the instrument would see the wisdom of this reasoning. **We know that using only vocal music is right. The simple appeal is why take chances then and use the instrument? It is not a mark of wisdom using it. It is foolishness and a presumptuous sin (Psa. 19:13).**

Arguments Used by Those Who Favor the Instrument

First, The Use of the Greek Word *psallo*

Abbot-Smith's Greek Lexicon define the word, "In the New Testament, to sing a hymn, sing praise." *Thayer's Greek Lexicon* defines it, "In the New Testament to sing a hymn, to celebrate the praise of God in song." The *Analytical Greek Lexicon* defines it, "In the New Testament to sing praises." F. F. Bruce said, "It is used in the New Testament with the meaning to sing psalms." *McClintock and Strong's Cyclopedia* states, "The Greek word [psallo] is applied among the Greeks of modern time exclusively to sacred music, which in the Eastern church has never been any other than vocal, instrument being unknown in that church, as it was in the primitive Church" (Vol. VII, p. 739). The Italian phrase *a cappella* also leads us to believe that *psallo* means vocal music only.

Arndt-Gingrich said that *psallo* meant "Sing exclusively, . . . with no reference to instrumental accompaniment" (*A Greek-English Lexicon To The New Testament*, p. 891, second edition, 1979).

Second, The Instrument Is an Aid

If the doctor tells you to eat jello, you will use a bowl and a spoon. Those items are aids. But, if you put cake in the bowl, that is an addition--not an aid. A pitch pipe is an aid. You cannot sing without pitch. A piano or organ is an addition--not an aid. We do not need a piano to obey the command to sing. One needs a bowl and a spoon to obey the doctor's orders to eat jello. A church building is an aid. Pews are aids. The public address system is an aid. It is interesting that choir teachers in public schools like to have those who attend the Churches of Christ sing in their choirs. Why? Very simply because they are better singers. Their voices have not been corrupted by the instrument and they can read music much better. Mark this down brethren--God is concerned with the obedience to the command and quality of our heart--not the vocal quality that we have. If you have to have good vocal quality to enter heaven, I am lost!!!

Third, David Used Instruments

Yes, David used them. Read 1 Chronicles 23:3-5 and 2 Chronicles 29:25-27 and Psalms 150. In the Old Testament, instruments in worship were a command of God. Yes, God approved it. But, let us ask the simple question, does this mean that we can use them today? David kept and observed the Sabbath Day, practiced circumcision as a religious rite, had to go through priests to approach God, practiced polygamy, offered animal sacrifices, etc. Just because David did something in the Old Testament which was right like offering animal sacrifices, does that mean it is right to do them today? Absolutely not! Just because David used musical instruments in worship to God, does not mean God approves of them today. We live by the New Testament--not the Old Testament (Heb. 8:1-13).

Fourth, There Are Harps in Heaven

This argument comes from the Book of Revelation. Listen to Revelation 1:1, "The Revelation of Jesus Christ, which God gave him to show unto his servants, even the things which must shortly come to pass: and he sent and **signified** it by his angel unto his servant John." The word **"signified"** means "to teach by signs and symbols and pictures." The Book of Revelation is a sign and symbol book. After Election Day if you see in the paper an elephant swinging a donkey by the tail, does anyone have to teach you what happened? The very first verse of the Book informs us not to take everything literally. The Book talks about heaven having streets of gold. Will there be literally streets of gold in heaven? No! Heaven is a spiritual place not a physical one.

Revelation 1:10 says, "I was in the Spirit on the Lord's day, and I heard behind me a great voice, **as** of a trumpet." This is a simile. A simile is a figure of speech expressing comparison or likeness by use of such terms as like or as. It was not a literal trumpet but the sound of a trumpet.

Revelation 4:1 discusses "a voice **as** of a trumpet." Again, this is a simile like Revelation 1:10.

Read Revelation 5:8. Will there literally be golden bowls in heaven? No. Will there literally be harps in heaven? No. Nothing physical is going to enter heaven.

Revelation 14:2 says, "And the voice which I heard was **as** the voice of harpers harping with their harps." Again, this is a simile, a figure of speech and is not supposed to be taken literally.

Revelation 15:2, "And I saw **as** it were a sea of glass . . . having harps of God." This is a simile where sounds are said to be like instruments but are not instruments themselves.

Fifth, The Popularity Argument

People say using instrumental music is the going thing. They say everybody is doing it. They say it appeals to people and draws a crowd. They say it is needed to bring in the people. But, God said a long time ago, "Thou shalt not follow a multitude to do evil; neither shalt thou speak in a cause to turn aside after a multitude to wrest justice" (Exodus 23:2). We live by what God says not what the majority says! We must learn that the majority does not determine right and wrong! Popularity does not make something right in the eyes of God. The message of Noah was not popular but it was right. The message of Jeremiah was not popular but it was right. The message of all the prophets was not popular but it was right. On the other hand, the message of Jeroboam was popular but it was not right. Jeroboam changed the location of worship, who to worship, the time of worship, and who was to lead in worship. It is sad but true that the majority of people will be lost eternally (Matt. 7:13-14). Therefore, we should not follow the majority. God's people have always been in the minority and that fact should not take us by surprise.

Sixth, The "I Like It" Argument

When Jeroboam told the North Israelites that they would not have to travel that long difficult journey to Jerusalem, they liked it. That message appealed to them. He was making it a lot easier for the people.

It is sad that today many worship in a certain way because it appeals to them. Very simply, they like it. It does not make any difference whether it is right or wrong in the eyes of God. What God has said goes out the window and is replaced with worship that is appealing. This is a far cry from what God through Samuel told Saul, "Behold, to obey is better than sacrifice" (1 Sam. 15:22). Paul condemned "will worship" (Col. 2:23). Will-worship is when man worships the way he wills-- not the way God wills!

Just because we like something, that does not justify its use. The basic, fundamental, bottom-line question should always be--"What does God want?" Remember the chapter on "Worship." We are to worship God "in spirit and truth" (John 4:24). We are to give to God in worship what He wants us to give to Him--not what we want to give to Him!

If I am going to give my wife a present, I am not likely to give her something because I like it or want it. I would not give her a set of golf clubs, a lawn mower, or a new Greek lexicon. I would find something she likes and wants. If I am going to offer something to God, and I want Him to be pleased with it, I have to offer what He has specified and what He wants.

Seventh, The Natural Talent Argument

Some people say that if one has a talent for playing the piano, he should be allowed to use that talent to glorify God. But, here again we go back to the basic and fundamental aspect of worship. We are to give God what He wants--not what we want to give to Him. The question must be does God want a piano used in worship to Him? Suppose a person has a talent for yodeling. Because he has that talent, does that make it right to use in worship? Absolutely not--because it is not worship in truth! There are hundreds of different kinds of talents that Christians have. But, that does not justify their use in worship. God also gave some the ability to throw a football and make three-point shots in basketball. Shall one do that in worship?

Conclusion

It seems popular today to argue, "I do not see any place where use of instrumental music is condemned in the New Testament." No one is arguing that anyone is going to find a "Thou shalt not use instrumental music in worship." The fundamental point of worship is that where the Lord gives a commandment, that eliminates doing anything else.

The New Testament does not pretend to contain a list of all the things people should not do in worship. It would be too voluminous to read if it did. In Galatians 5:19-21 Paul gives a list of sins that will keep people out of heaven. At the end of verse 22 he adds "and such like." In other words, the list is not an exhaustive, complete list of sins. Popes, cardinals, bishops are not prohibited by a specific, "Thou shalt not have" in the New Testament. Nor are infant baptism, sprinkling for baptism, use of incense, dancing, and many other practices. But, none of them are authorized. One must ask the question, "Where does the New Testament authorize a practice?"

I find it tragic and ironical that just at the time many of our brethren seem ready to adopt instrumental music, a preacher from the Reformed Presbyterian Church has come out with an attack on its use as not having scriptural authority (cf. Brian Schwertley, ***Musical Instruments in the Public Worship of God***). Jack Lewis wrote, "Though there is no reason to think Schwertley was influenced by our preachers or by our practice, one could hardly improve on the argument he gives. One would hope that Schwertley's trampling on a few other pet trends will not keep Bible believers from at least considering his reasoning."

For Thought or Discussion

1. What is the Law of Inclusion and Exclusion? How does this relate to the Instrumental Music question?
2. Discuss aids and additions from the commands given by God to Noah and Moses.
3. What is the difference between an acceptable "aid" in worship and a sinful "addition" in worship?
4. Would it be permissible to use Fritos and Coca-Cola instead of unleavened bread and fruit of the vine? Why?
5. What did Tom Lawson say about Instrumental Music? Why is what he said important?

6. What are the simple appeal and the simple question presented by John Hobbs? Do you agree? Why?

7. Define the Greek word *psallo*.

8. (True or False) Using the instrument makes one a better singer.

9. (True or False) God is more concerned with our vocal quality than obedience to His command.

10. (True or False) What David did in the Old Testament (like using instrumental music) proves it is acceptable to do today. Why?

11. Explain the word "signified" in Revelation 1:1. How does this word relate to the entire Book of Revelation?

12. What is the fundamental question in worshipping God?

13. (True or False) The New Testament gives a complete list of things Christians must not do. Scripture?

14. What is significant about Brian Schwertley's book?

15. Discuss the use of instruments in the Book of Revelation.

16. Do you believe there will be literally harps in heaven? Why?

17. (True or False) The Book of Revelation uses figures of speech like similes.

18. What is the significance of the Italian phrase *a cappella*?

9

The Teaching of the New Testament on Baptism #1

Baptism is very important in the Christian faith. Sadly, many people have twisted, perverted, distorted, and wrested the true meaning of baptism (2 Pet. 3:15-17). Many want to de-hydrate the Bible and take baptism out of the salvation process. In this chapter and the next we will seek to set forth what the New Testament teaches on this subject.

Who Do You Baptize?

The Catholics, Lutherans, Presbyterians, Methodists, and others say babies should be baptized. The reason these religious groups and others baptize babies is because they believe in Hereditary Total Depravity. Up until 1850 virtually all Baptist groups believed in Hereditary Total Depravity. The Baptist Charles Spurgeon believed in this doctrine. This doctrine says that babies are born sinners, totally depraved of anything good and are therefore damned to hell.

Several years ago I was preaching in San Angelo, Texas. I met a woman who grew up in a non-religious home. I asked her about her mother. She said her mother was a member of the Lutheran church. She gave birth to a baby boy who only lived a few hours. She went to her Lutheran minister and asked him to perform a funeral service for her infant son. He absolutely refused. She asked him why? He responded, "Your son is damned to an eternal hell of fire and there is not one thing you or I can do about it." (I have heard about this happening in the Catholic Church as well.) Sadly, unfortunately, the mother went into a deep depression from which she never recovered. She never darkened the door of a Lutheran church again or any other church. There are two main problems. First, the mother believed what she was told. She should have studied the Bible for herself and realized that babies are not born sinners (Ezek. 18:20; Eph. 5:17; 2 Tim. 2:15). Her Lutheran minister had taught false doctrine. Sadly, she believed it. Her belief of false doctrine led her to a course of action to never enter a church building again. Second, babies are not to be baptized--only those old enough to hear, understand and comprehend the truth of Scripture are to be baptized. Technically, baptism is by immersion--it is not sprinkling or pouring.

This leads us to ask the question--Are babies born sinners? Are babies born totally depraved? I would encourage you to read my book *Advanced Bible Study* where I deal with the four main Scriptures that false teachers use to advance and promote this false doctrine. In this chapter we will examine the one key verse they distort--Psalms 51:5. The other three are: Psalms 58:3 and Ephesians 2:3 and Romans 5:12.

Hereditary Total Depravity

Dr. Ralph Gore, the Dean of Theology at the Trinity Theological Seminary, says, "In Adam's sin we all died, even those who have not reached the age of accountability. Even infants nonetheless died because they were guilty of Adam's sin and the guilt of Adam's sin had been imputed to them although individually they had not voluntarily violated the will of God." He also said, "We became sinners as a result of inheriting the corruption of nature from Adam . . . Since every part of our nature has been affected by sin, man can do nothing to move toward God." This is the first cardinal point of Calvinism--people are born totally depraved and born sinners. Since Calvinists tie baptism to salvation from sin, they want to sprinkle babies and call that baptism.

Psalms 51:5

Probably the most important biblical passage used by Calvinists to support the doctrine of Hereditary Total Depravity is Psalms 51:5.

Psalms 51:5 (ASV)--"Behold, I was brought forth in iniquity; and in sin did my mother conceive me."

Psalms 51:5 (Dr. Klein)--"Look, in iniquity I was brought forth, and in sin my mother conceived me." Dr. Klein is a Baptist Hebrew professor. He said, "I don't think the passage speaks to original sin. Some people read into the passage things that are not there."

Psalms 51:5 (NIV)--"Surely I was sinful at birth, sinful from the time my mother conceived me."

The NIV translation of Psalms 51:5 leads people to believe in the doctrine of Hereditary Total Depravity. The NIV translation has many problems! Many of those on the translating committee were Calvinists and as a result they incorporated their Calvinistic doctrine into God's word and perverted it! One of my Greek teachers was on the committee. I am not saying they made a mistake on every verse but they did on many passages. For example, the NIV translates John 3:16 as "Shall not perish." The verse should read "Should not perish." The Greek verb "perish" is in the subjunctive mood--not the indicative mood. The Greek subjunctive mood is the mood of possibility not actuality. Therefore, the ASV and KJV are correct while the NIV and NASV (1995) are wrong.

Martin Kaufman, a pastor of a Lutheran church in Cisco, Texas, wrote, "The Bible speaks very clearly in Psalms 51:5 that even before a person is born, from the moment of conception, that person is sinful." Is this right? Absolutely not! Here are **seven reasons** why Psalms 51:5 does not teach a baby is born a sinner.

First, the verse is an example of Hebrew poetry. Poetry abounds with bold figures of speech and a freedom of expression that departs from normal usage. It is a great mistake to extract statements from poetry and consider them as foundational bases of doctrinal systems. Poetry is not to be understood in a strict literal way! In an equally poetic passage, Job 31:16-18, Job is denying the charge of his adversaries that he neglected taking care of widows and orphans. Job says he cared for the orphan and widow "from my mother's womb" (Job 31:18). Obviously no one believes that on the day of his birth he took care of the orphan and widow. This verse is highly figurative, employing poetic license. The point made by Job is as far as back as he can remember he has been mindful of the less fortunate.

Second, consider a study of Acts 2:8. Acts 2:8 says, "And how hear we, every man in our own language wherein we were born?" Does this mean that they were born automatically speaking a language? Obviously not! No baby is literally born speaking a language. Acts 2:8 means they were born in a geographical area or country that spoke a certain language. The same analysis applies to Psalms 51:5. David was teaching in this verse that he was born into a world of sin, a sinful environment just like a man is born into an area speaking a certain language.

Third, consider a study of the phrase "In sin did my mother conceive me." If someone said, "In drunkenness my husband beat me." Would anyone attribute drunkenness to the wife? No! If someone said, "In anger my father beat me." Would anyone attribute anger to the child? No! So, when David said, "In sin did my mother conceive me"--sin is not being attributed to the child! The child is not a sinner!

Fourth, consider a study of Ezekiel 18:20. This verse states, "The soul that sinneth, it shall die: the son shall not bear the iniquity of the father, neither shall the father bear the iniquity of the son; the righteousness of the righteous shall be upon him, and the wickedness of the wicked shall be upon him." Here is a clear verse that teaches children do not inherit sin or iniquity from their parents. A person is righteous or wicked based on what he himself has done or not done! The apostle John wrote, "He that doeth righteousness is righteous" (1 John 3:7). It is most unfortunate that many scholars ignore or misuse Ezekiel 18:20. Calvinists like Erickson, Enns, Gore, and others play "Passover" with this verse. Could a verse be plainer? Could it be more straightforward?

Fifth, this verse is an idiom. Dr. John Willis wrote, "The best explanation is that the poet is using as ancient Near Eastern meaning that he, like all human beings, was prone or inclined to sin from his youth up, because he was constantly surrounded by sin and temptation" (Consider Psalms 22:9-10; 71:6).

Sixth, examine the context of Psalms 51:5. David's focus in the Psalm is his own sins. Notice he says: "my transgressions" (51:1) and "mine iniquities" (51:2) and "my sin" (51:2) and "my transgressions" (51:3) and "my sin" (51:3) and "I have sinned" (51:4) and "done that which is evil" (51:4). David clearly understood that sin was an action on his part. He was not saying he was a sinner because he was born that way. He was a sinner because he participated in sin.

Seventh, one must study the entire Bible. God's word harmonizes in all of its parts. The Bible absolutely does not teach Hereditary Total Depravity! Many times children do suffer for the consequences of their parents sins (Exodus 20:5) but never the guilt of the parent's iniquity (Ezek. 18:20). Paul said, "I was alive apart from the law once" (Rom. 7:9). Paul was not talking about physical life in Romans 7:9. He was discussing spiritual life. When was he alive apart from the law? When he was a baby!

Guilt, iniquity, and sin are not transferrable through the blood lines. It is a great sin to distort, pervert, twist, and wrest the meaning of Scripture! Those who do so--do it unto their own destruction (2 Peter 3:15-17). The point is we do not baptize babies because they are not sinners. They are in a safe state until they reach the age of accountability (Romans 7:9).

The Problem We Face Concerning Baptism

Many people say you can baptize one of three ways—sprinkling, pouring, or immersion. If you ask a person, have you been baptized? He might say "yes." But, in his mind, if he was sprinkled, he was baptized. In his mind, if he was poured on, he was baptized. Therefore, we have a problem. The Catholics, Presbyterians, Lutherans, Methodists, and other religious groups sprinkle and call that baptism. *Webster's New World College Dictionary* 1997 defines baptism as "The ceremony or sacrament of admitting a person into Christianity or a specific Christian church by immersing the individual in water or by pouring or sprinkling water on the individual" (p. 109). But, we must remember that Webster gives the current English definition of the word, how it is used in modern English. It is interesting that the same dictionary defines the original Greek word as "immersion." What we want is to define the word baptism according to Greek authorities--not by a modern English dictionary.

The Meaning of the Greek Word *Baptizo*

Thayer's Lexicon defines *baptizo*, "An immersion in water, performed as a sign of the removal of sin, and administered to those who, impelled by a desire for salvation, sought admission to the benefits of Messiah's kingdom. To dip, submerge, cleanse by dipping" (p. 94). *Arndt and Gingrich Lexicon* says, "Dip, immerse, wash, plunge, sink, overwhelm" (2nd ed., p.131). **Abbott-Smith** says, "To dip, immerse sink; of ablution, immersion as a religious rite" (p. 74). *The Analytical Greek Lexicon* states, "To dip, immerse, cleanse or purify by washing" (p. 65). *Kittel's Theological Dictionary of the New Testament* states, "*Baptizo* occurs in the sense of immerse" (Vol. I, p. 530). **Bullinger** defines it, "To immerse for a religious purpose. Immersion or washing with water, washing unto purification from sin." *Liddell and Scott Lexicon* says, "Dipping in water, immersion." **W. E. Vine** states, "Consists of the processes of immersion, submersion and emergence." **G. R. Beasley-Murray** defines it, "Dip, immerse, submerge." *The Encyclopedia of Bible Words* states, "From earliest times it was used in the sense of immersing" (p. 101). *The New Catholic Encyclopedia*, Vol. 2, 1967, pages 56-57 states, "It is evident that baptism in the early church was by immersion. This is implicit in terminology and context." *The Old Catholic Encyclopedia*, Vol. 2, 1907, pages 261-262 states, "The most ancient form usually employed was unquestionably immersion. This is not only evident from the writings of the Fathers and the early rituals of both Latin and Oriental Churches, but it can also be gathered from the Epistles of St. Paul." In the book *Martin Luther*

(*Selections from His Writings*) edited by John Dillenberger, 1961, page 300 Luther himself wrote, "For the Greek word *baptizo* means immerse or plunge, and the word *baptizma* means immersion." In John Calvin's *Institutes*, book 4, chapter 15, page 599, Calvin said, "The very word baptize, however, signifies to immerse; and it is certain that immersion was the practice of the ancient church." Philip Schaff, a Presbyterian, wrote in *History of the Christian Church*, Vol. 1, 1884, page 648, "The usual form of baptism was immersion. This is inferred from the original meaning of the Greek *baptizein* and *baptismos*." Conybeare and Howson, members of the Church of England, in *Life and Epistles of St. Paul*, 1862, Vol. 2, page 209, wrote, "Primitive baptism was by immersion." Based on this overwhelming evidence, there should be no question to the sincere person seeking truth. Baptism is immersion!

The KJV and the Word Baptism

In 1604, King James commissioned the making of a new translation. It would be called the King James Version. King James believed in sprinkling--not immersion. When the scholars came to the Greek word *baptizo*, they were in a dilemma. If they translate it immersion, King James would not like that. They might even lose their heads. In those days people were killed for religious reasons. If they translate it sprinkling or pouring, that would not be accurate scholarship. The Greek word *rhantizo* means sprinkle and the Greek word *cheo* means pour. So, what the translators did was to transliterate the word. They just brought the Greek letters over into the English and made an English word out of the Greek word *baptizo*. Thus, the translators kept their heads and their scholarship.

Examining Four Important Key Bible Verses

John 3:23, "And John also was baptizing in Aenon near to Salim, because there was **much water**." Please notice why John was baptizing in Aenon near to Salim-- because there was **"much water"** there!! You do not need much water to sprinkle or pour. This very clear fact alone supports the view that baptism means immersion!

Acts 8:38, "They both went down into the water, both Philip and the Eunuch; and he baptized him." Notice they both went down into the water. The biblical example of baptism is both going down into the water. Thus baptism is not sprinkling or pouring.

Also consider Romans 6:3-4 and Colossians 2:12. Both of these verses picture baptism as a "burial" and being "raised" which requires much water.

A Pointed Question Concerning Baptism

Since the evidence for the meaning of baptism is overwhelmingly convincing, how can religious people today accept sprinkling for immersion? Sadly, the answer is really quite simple. Some people believe (and falsely I might add) that Webster's English Dictionary supports the view. Some people believe you can substitute Fritos and Coca-Cola in the Lord's Supper for unleavened bread and fruit of the vine. This is where I, along with many other strong conservative brethren, part company with many people. It is a "presumptuous" sin (Psa. 19:13) to sprinkle and call that baptism. Sprinkling is not baptism. To believe so is pure ignorance! **I do not care about being on the side of the majority. I want to be on the side of the truth!** Jesus said, "The truth shall set you free" (John 8:32). If people criticize me, that is just fine. Jesus said, "Woe unto you, when all men shall speak well of you!" (Luke 6:26). If we are not receiving opposition for our teaching, we better check what we are teaching. If we teach the truth, some are not going to like it (2 Tim. 4:1-5)!

An Event in Church History

Eusebius, an early church historian, sets forth the first recorded case of sprinkling for baptism. It occurred around 251 A. D. Eusebius wrote, "Novation, . . . it being supposed that he would die, received baptism, being sprinkled with water on the bed where he lay, if that be called baptism." Even Eusebius questioned calling sprinkling baptism. Can we change what God has required and commanded? Absolutely not! It is sin to think so. We must worship the Lord "in spirit and truth" (John 4:24). Thus, the teaching of the New Testament is one who has been sprinkled has not been immersed. He has not been baptized even if he thinks he has! **Anyone who says the "mode" of baptism is unimportant is making an eternal mistake. We commit sin if we try to change what God has legislated!**

Conclusion

Nadab and Abihu substituted "strange fire" for the correct fire and died on the spot. Would Noah have obeyed God if he substituted some type of wood for gopher wood? No! Would Moses have been obedient if he substituted some type of wood for the Ark of the Covenant instead of using acacia wood? No! Would Naaman have been cleansed of his leprosy if he went to some other river than the river Jordan? No! Jesus told the man born blind in John 9 to go wash in the Pool of Siloam and he would be healed. Could the blind man have gone to some other pool? No! **When God tells us what to do, we are not free to substitute! I pray that all of God's people would learn this extremely important fact.**

For Thought or Discussion

1. Is it possible to twist and distort Scripture to one's own destruction? (2 Pet. 3:15-17). What does this strongly imply?
2. Why do people think that babies need to be baptized?
3. (True or False) Each person must study the Bible for himself to discover the truth of God's word. Scripture?
4. (True or False) Calvinists believe that babies in the womb are guilty of sin. What verse in the Bible clears this problem?
5. What does the NIV translation of Psalms 51:5 teach? Is it right or wrong?
6. Discuss Psalms 51:5 in-depth.
7. What is the problem with Webster's English Dictionary as it relates to the meaning of baptism?
8. How does Greek scholarship define the word *baptizo*?
9. How did the KJV translators handle the Greek word *baptizo*? Why?

10. What does John 3:23 teach about the meaning of baptism?

11. (True or False) Faithful Christians should live a life that will not bring any criticism or opposition. Why?

12. What happened in 251 A.D. as it relates to baptism? Does this example prove that one can substitute sprinkling for baptism?

13. (True or False) The mode of worship is just as important as the purpose of heart, attitude, sincerity, and intent of worship. (John 4:24)

14. What do you think about the Lutheran minister who refused to perform the funeral of the baby boy who died a few hours after childbirth?

15. How should John 3:16 be translated?

10

The Teaching of the New Testament on Baptism #2

There Is No Such Person as an Unbaptized Christian

Richard Baggett was an instructor at the Sunset School of Preaching in Lubbock, Texas. Richard said, "The first sign of liberalism is to deny that baptism is the identifying mark of a Christian." Richard was right!

In Romans 6:3 Paul wrote, "Or are ye ignorant that **all we** who were baptized into Christ Jesus were baptized into his death?" Who are the **"we"** in the verse? Christians. How many Christians have been baptized? Paul said **"all."**

In 1 Corinthians 12:13 Paul wrote, "For by one Spirit were **we all** baptized into one body." Who are the **"we"** in the verse? Christians. How many Christians have been baptized? Paul said **"all."**

In my opinion the strongest evidence for the fact that there is no such person as an unbaptized Christian are the cases of conversion in the Book of Acts. There are ten cases of conversion in Acts where specific details of their conversion are given. Here they are: Pentecost (Acts 2:38-41), Samaritans (Acts 8:12), Simon (Acts 8:13), Eunuch (Acts 8:26-40), Saul (Acts 9:18; 22:16), Cornelius (Acts 10: 47-48), Lydia (Acts 16:15), Jailor

(Acts 16:30-34), the Corinthians (Acts 18:8), and the twelve (Acts 19:1-7). The significant detail is that baptism is given in all ten cases! Why? Very simply, one cannot be saved and become a Christian unless he has been baptized. Baptism is the final step that takes a person outside of Christ and puts him into Christ (Rom. 6:3-4; 1 Cor. 12:13; Gal. 3:26-27) where salvation is (2 Tim. 2:10; Eph. 1:3).

The highly-respected scholar F. F. Bruce wrote, **"The idea of an unbaptized Christian is simply not entertained in the New Testament"** (*The Book of Acts*, p. 77).

Church historian Michael Svigel wrote, "People in the New Testament and in the early church responded to the gospel not by coming forward during an invitation, by praying a 'sinner's prayer,' or by raising their hand with their eyes closed and head bowed--but by confessing their faith before others and submitting to water baptism. There was such a close, sometimes immediate, chronological relationship between belief, repentance, confession, conversion, and baptism that these terms were often used interchangeably, and **it was inconceivable that a person would be considered a 'Christian' without being baptized"** (*Heroes and Heretics: Solving the Modern Mystery of the Ancient Church*, p. 21).

Church historian John Hannah wrote, "The church was viewed as the ark of salvation; to be saved, one had to be a member of it through baptism . . . **Baptism was seen as the entrance into spiritual life**, a view derived from several passages of Scripture (Mark 16:16; John

3:5; Acts 2:38, 22:16; Titus 3:5). Water baptism and life from death were seen as a unity, occurring together, not separate from each other" (*The Kregel Pictorial Guide to Church History*, p. 16). Please note that Hannah says that baptism is understood to be "the entrance into spiritual life." But, if baptism is the very way in which one enters spiritual life how could one come into possession of life apart from baptism? Thus, no one can be saved and be a Christian without being baptized!

Baptism Must Be Done in Spirit (John 4:24)

Jesus said, "God is Spirit: and they that worship him must worship in spirit and truth." The word "must" means it is absolutely necessary. To worship "in spirit" means "to have the right purpose of heart, sincerity of heart, the right attitude, the right intent, and the right motive." **The purpose for which something is done is just as important as the act itself.** Consider these examples:

In 1 Corinthians 13:3, Paul said, "And if I bestow all my goods to feed the poor, and if I give my body to be burned, but have not love, it profiteth me nothing." In other words, if our motive is not right, the act is worthless.

In Acts 19:1-7, we find the story of the twelve men who had received the baptism of John but not Christian baptism. Note both baptisms were done by immersion. But, John's baptism looked forward to the coming of Christ. Christian baptism looks to the cross and what Jesus accomplished in his death! When the Day of Pentecost came, John's baptism was invalid. Therefore, one had to receive Christian baptism. These twelve men "were baptized into the name of the Lord Jesus" (Acts 19:5; cf. Matt. 28:19). The phrase "into the name of" means "into the possession of." Notice these twelve men were immersed twice but for different reasons. When Paul taught them the truth about Christian baptism, their reason and motive and purpose for being baptized changed. **This teaches the necessity of having the right motive in being baptized!**

In Matthew 6:1 Jesus said, "Take heed that ye do not your righteousness before men, to be seen of them: else ye have no reward with your Father who is in heaven." If our righteous acts are done "before men, to be seen of them," then our righteous acts are worthless in the eyes of God. Again Jesus is teaching that we must have the right motive and right purpose for the act to be acceptable before God! **The purpose for which something is done is just as important as the act itself.**

When it comes to baptism, one must do it "unto the remission of sins" (Acts 2:38), to be saved (Mark 16:16; 1 Peter 3:21), to wash away sins (Acts 22:16), and to come into Christ where salvation is (Rom. 6:3-4; Gal. 3:27; 1 Cor. 12:13; Eph. 1:3; 2 Tim. 2:10). Baptism is a "must" (Acts 9:6; 22:16). It is not optional. Baptism is "unto the remission of sins." Baptism is not because one's sins have already been remitted. One Baptist preacher said, "I wouldn't baptize someone unless he was saved already." This is false doctrine! One is not saved then baptized! In Mark 16:16 Jesus said, "He that believeth (Aorist tense participle) and is baptized (Aorist tense participle) shall be saved (Future tense--main verb)." The rule of New Testament Greek grammar is that the aorist tense participle describes action that takes place either antecedent (before) or simultaneous (same time) to the main verb but never subsequent (after). Therefore, one is baptized at the same time he is saved never after he is saved! If one is baptized and it is not for the right reason, then that baptism is ineffective and invalid and worthless! We must not change what God requires. **The purpose for baptism must be for the right reason.**

False Teaching by Some Members of the Church of Christ

Dr. Paul Southern penned an article entitled "Winds of Change" wherein he deplored the fact that "some are beginning to doubt the importance of baptism" (***Christian Journal***, June 1995, p. 2).

It breaks our hearts to consider the words we find in Rubel Shelly's and John York's ***The Jesus Proposal*** (Siloam Springs, AR: Leafwood Publishers, 2003). On pages 172-174, the organist of a denomination asked about the validity of her "baptism" ((i.e. her being sprinkled and not immersed). She asked, "Do you regard me as a Christian? Do you count me as your sister in Christ? Or do you think I am lost and need to be saved?" Please notice carefully the response they gave! They said, "Of course I see you as a Christian! And I am sorry you have apparently met somebody from a Church of Christ or some other immersionist group who treated you otherwise . . . So, yes, I see the two of us as equals and peers. We are brother and sister to each other in the one great family or church of the living God . . . And, no I don't think you are lost." Shelly and York are committing a presumptuous sin when they say sprinkling is an acceptable substitute for immersion. **The "mode" of baptism must be followed (John 4:24).** What makes them think they have the right to change what God has legislated? They do not have that right! No one does! God's word will not allow it. This lady was rhantized not baptized! Thus, according to the Scriptures, she is not saved (Mark 16:16; Acts 2:38; Acts 22:16; and 1 Peter 3:21).

Max Lucado is a false teacher. In a December 1996 radio speech he taught false doctrine. He basically encouraged people to say the sinner's prayer and for him that was sufficient for salvation. He told people to pray, "Father, I give my heart to you. I give you my sins. I give you my tears, I give you my fears, I give you my whole life. I accept the gift of your Son on the cross for my sins. And I ask you Father, to receive me as your child through Jesus I pray." Then he went on to say, "I want to encourage you to find a church. I want to encourage you to be baptized. I want to encourage you to read your Bible. But, I don't want you to do any of that so that you will be saved. I want you to do that because you are saved."

In *The San Antonio Express-News* newspaper of September 6, 2003, Max Lucado said, "Oak Hills also believes salvation doesn't come through baptism, but that baptism is the initial step of obedience after salvation." Clearly, Max is teaching false doctrine. Max is definitely not a Church historian or a Bible scholar and is certainly not a Greek scholar. Truth is not on his side! Max Lucado and Rubel Shelly and John York and others are right in their own eyes. They are not right in the eyes of

God (Prov. 3:5-7; 23:4; 28:26; Isa. 5:21). Romans 16:17 teaches false teachers should be marked and avoided.

Several years ago I had a discussion with one who thought that Rubel Shelly was a great Christian because of his sincerity. But, brethren, sincerity alone does not make one right with God (cf. Rom. 10:1-3; Acts 23:1). I would encourage the reader to obtain my book *Searching for Biblical Truth* and read chapters 9 and 10 and 13. In this book I answer the arguments that baptism is not the point of salvation. I also examine some of the technical New Testament Greek points that some ignorant people want to use.

A Study of Romans 6:3-4

In Romans 6:3-4 the apostle Paul wrote, "Or are ye ignorant that all we who were baptized into Christ Jesus were **baptized into his death**? We were **buried therefore with him through baptism into death**: that like as Christ was raised from the dead through the glory of the Father, so we also might **walk in newness of life**." What does it mean to be "baptized into his death?" It means to be baptized into the saving effects of His death! We are "loosed from our sins by his **blood**" (Rev. 1:5). We have been "purchased with his own **blood**" (Acts 20:28). We are "justified by his **blood**" (Rom. 5:9). "We have our redemption through his **blood**" (Eph. 1:7). We were redeemed "with precious **blood**, as of a lamb without blemish and without spot, even the **blood** of Christ" (1 Pet. 1:18-19). Jesus brought peace between God and man "through the **blood** of his cross" (Col. 1:20). "If we walk in the light, we have fellowship one with another, and the **blood** of Jesus his Son cleanseth us from all sin" (1 John 1:7). We have boldness to enter into God's presence "by the **blood** of Jesus" (Heb. 10:19). Jesus "through his own **blood,** entered in once for all into the holy place, having obtained eternal redemption" (Heb. 9:12). Can one be saved without the blood of Jesus covering his sins? Absolutely not! It is at the point of baptism that one comes into contact with the saving blood of Jesus Christ.

Notice the text says "we were buried." Let me ask a simple question? Do you bury dead people or live people? Very simply you bury dead people. Before a person goes down into the watery grave of baptism, he is dead spiritually. When he is immersed, he comes into contact with the blood of Jesus. He is baptized into his death. Then when he arises out of the watery tomb, he is to live in "newness of life." Please notice that the newness of life can not start until he is buried with Jesus in the act of baptism. Therefore, baptism is a necessary and indispensible part of the salvation process.

A Study of Romans 6:17-18

In Romans 6:17-18 Paul wrote, "But thanks be to God, that, whereas ye were servants of sin, ye **became obedient from the heart** to that **form of teaching** whereunto ye were delivered: and **being *then* made free from sin**, ye became servants of righteousness." Here is a simple question. When is one made free from sin? It is when he obeys from the heart that form or pattern of teaching that was delivered! It is not when he prays the "sinner's prayer." The words "became obedient" are from an Aorist tense indicative verb. The Aorist tense describes point action. The words "from the heart" indicate the right reason, the right purpose, sincerity of heart. It is equivalent to worshipping God "in spirit." The word "form" is from the Greek word *tupos* which means pattern, a mold that produces the same result. The "form of teaching" in context is obviously baptism. Romans 6 deals with dying to self and being baptized into Christ and being baptized into his death. The "form" of Romans 6 is basically equivalent to worshipping God in "truth." In other words, the form or pattern is baptism which means immersion. **Please, please, please notice it is at the point of obedience of baptism that one is then made free from sin! Not before! This is the truth of Scripture! We did not write the Bible!** We, those in the Church of Christ, do not believe that the water saves anyone! It is the blood of Jesus that saves us. But, Romans 6:17-18 teaches the blood saves us when we are obedient with the right purpose and right mode. Both elements are necessary. One is not more important than the other.

Baptized at Night?

Some religious groups wait several months before baptizing those desiring it. Why? Because they do not believe that baptism has anything to do with one's salvation. But, in the New Testament we find a different view. Acts 16:33 states, "And he took them the same hour of the night, and washed their stripes; and was baptized, he and all his, immediately." Why baptize at night time? Why the immediate nature of baptism? Because one is not saved before he is baptized. One cannot be a Christian without being baptized (Rom. 6:3; 1Cor. 12:13). One is saved at the point of baptism (Rom. 6:17-18). Hence, there is the need to baptize at night. I have baptized people during the middle of the night at the building. I have also witnessed others who were baptized during the middle of the night. Why? The New Testament clearly teaches that baptism is necessary for salvation.

Conclusion

Sadly, we have some in the Churches of Christ that are teaching error on baptism and other biblical subjects. We must **"Ask for the Old Paths"** and walk therein! We must come to the conclusion that being a true follower of Jesus sets us apart from others. God's people are in the minority and will always be in the minority (Matt. 7:13-14).

The New Testament teaches that baptism is the point of salvation. It is not the cause. The cause is the blood of Jesus. But, we come into contact with the blood of Jesus when we are baptized (Rom. 6:3-4). We do not believe the water saves anyone. But, the water is the channel of obedience through which we can be saved. There are many examples in the Bible that teach this principle. Consider taking the city of Jericho, Naaman being healed, and the blind man in John 9 who was told to wash in the Pool of Siloam. The commands given to these people and their obedience were not the cause of blessing. The cause of being blessed was the power of God. But, the power of God became operative only when they obeyed!

For Thought or Discussion

1. What did Richard Baggett say was the first sign of liberalism? Do you agree? Why?
2. Explain how the New Testament teaches that there is no such person as an unbaptized Christian.
3. What did Bruce and Svigel say about a Christian and baptism?
4. Using Scripture discuss the concept that the purpose for which something is done is just as important as the act itself.
5. Using Mark 16:16 what is the force of New Testament Greek grammar.
6. (True or False) The purpose of baptism is inconsequential.
7. Why are Shelly and York and Lucado false teachers?
8. What verse in the New Testament teaches false teachers should be marked and avoided?
9. Where in the New Testament does it teach the sinner's prayer for salvation?
10. What is significant about the 10 cases of conversion in the Book of Acts?
11. (True or False) The mode of baptism is unimportant.
12. What does it mean we are "baptized into his (i.e. Jesus') death?"
13. (True or False) Before one can live a newness of spiritual life, he must first be buried with Jesus through baptism unto death.
14. Do you bury dead people or live people? From Romans 6, what is this teaching?
15. When is one made free from sin? Scripture?

16. (True or False) The water of baptism saved us.
17. (True or False) The water of baptism is the means through which our obedience brings salvation.
18. (True or False) The New Testament teaches one can and should wait several months before being baptized so the church can draw a large crowd.

11

"Why Churches of Christ Were Right After All"

Ted Campbell is an associate professor of church history at Southern Methodist University in Dallas, Texas. He posted on his blog an article with the headline "Why Churches of Christ Were Right After All." I will not reproduce his entire article. You can read the entire post at heartcoremethodist.org.

Dr. Campbell said, "I did not have a very positive impression of the Churches of Christ, but I'm beginning to change my mind, and now I'm thinking they may be right on some points that have distinguished them." He visited the Preston Road Church of Christ on March 6, 2011 and made several observations.

Dr. Campbell gives five reasons why the Churches of Christ may be right after all. **First, they have a profound insight into Christian music and its place in worship.** He said, "They sure do sing well and, speaking as a man on this point, I really appreciate a church that does not expect me to sing soprano, even transposed an octave lower. There's something utterly wonderful about the sound of human voices blending together in harmony. I wonder if we have gone too far with our instrumental fetish in worship."

The reason we "have a profound insight into Christian music and its place in worship" is very simple. That reason is we are following the teaching of the New Testament. When we do things God's way, God will bless us. When we do not obey God, He will chastise us (Deut. 28-30; Lev. 26; John 3:36; Romans 2:5-9). When Judah was living in sin, God pleaded with His people to return to the Old Paths. **Jeremiah 6:16 states, "Thus saith Jehovah, Stand ye in the ways and see, and ask for the old paths, where is the good way; and walk therein, and ye shall find rest for your souls: but they said, We will not walk therein."** The reason God pleaded with His people to return to the Old Paths was because of His "great love" for them. We must never lose sight of God's love for us! God said, "I have loved thee with an everlasting love: therefore with loving kindness have I drawn thee" (Jer. 31:3). Isaiah 63:9 states, "In all their affliction he was afflicted, and the angel of his presence saved them: **in his love and in his pity he redeemed them; and he bare them, and carried them all the days of old**." The apostle Paul said, "But God, being rich in mercy, for his **great love** wherewith he loved us" (Eph. 2:4). Paul also said, **"But God commended his own love toward us, in that, while we were yet sinners, Christ died for us"** (Rom. 5:8). John said, "Herein is love, not that we loved God, but that **he loved us, and sent his Son to be the propitiation for our sins"** (1 John 4:10).

Notice that Dr. Campbell said, "There's something utterly wonderful about the sound of human voices blending together in harmony." I firmly believe this is because God designed it this way. I hear Campbell's comment all the time from many people outside the Church of Christ. Public school choir teachers want students who attend Churches of Christ in their choir over other students. Why? They are just better singers. Their voices have not been corrupted by the instrument. Unbiased observation reveals that singing with an instrument hinders and discourages congregational singing. M. Krantz, teacher in the Conservatory of Music in Dresden, Germany, said, "We cannot possibly advise the use of instruments in connection with voice culture, for they are always a detriment, and create a state of dependency" (*Hunt-Inman Debate*, p. 54). "That vocal music is in general more expressive than the mechanically produced tone of instruments is undeniable. Religious feeling finds its most natural expression in vocal utterance for the human heart is the source of both devotion and song" (*Cath. Ency.* Vol. X, p. 651).

Second, Dr. Campbell says Churches of Christ "sure got the right name." He goes on to say, "Like the New Testament, they just name their congregations for the places where they meet, kind of like hobbits who built a new row of houses and then after a long discussion decided to name it 'New Row.' Perfectly straightforward. What's not to like about that?"

Reference to the Church of the New Testament is made by several designations. We do not insist that Christ's Church was called by one uniform name--it was not. However, each reference to the church is not without meaning; and we contend that in order to be scriptural a scriptural designation must be used. In referring to a number of local congregations, Paul says, "The churches of Christ salute you" (Rom. 16:16). The

Church belongs to Christ, and He sustains such a close relationship to it that it is proper, fitting, and scriptural to just call it "The Church of Christ." The Church of Christ belongs to him (Matt. 16:18); He built it (Matt. 16:18); He is the head of it (Col. 1:18); He is the foundation (1 Cor. 3:11); He purchased it with His own blood (Acts 20:28); it is His body (Eph. 1:22-23); He is the Savior of it (Eph. 5:23); He is the King over his Kingdom, which is His Church (Matt. 16:19; John 18:36).

Third, Dr. Campbell says, "The Churches of Christ celebrate the Lord's Supper every Sunday. Churches of Christ haven't fallen for Protestants' quirky idea that words can suffice in place of bread and wine. The service at Preston Road was very simple, with an elder of the congregation offering a simple prayer of thanksgiving for the bread and a prayer of thanksgiving for the wine, then the elements were distributed to the congregation in the pews. It reminded me a lot of the simple prayers over the bread and the wine in the second-century Didache document. I wondered if the distinguished second-century scholar Everett Ferguson of Abilene Christian University has somehow influenced this congregation or its leaders."

The New Testament and church history teach we are to partake of the Lord's Supper every Sunday (Acts 20:7; 1 Cor. 11:26; 1 Cor. 16:1-2). Some people say it will lose its meaning if you do it every week and therefore they elect to observe it once a quarter or once a year. But, brethren, we are not to follow what we think. We are to follow what God has said! It is a matter of obedience to God's word that we observe the Lord's Supper on the first day of every week. If you kiss your wife only once a week, will it lose its meaning? There are some in the Churches of Christ who say the Lord's Supper can be observed on Tuesday night or Saturday night. These brethren are in error and teaching false doctrine. They are not following the pattern set forth in the New Testament. We live by what God says not by what He does not say (Matt. 4:4)!

Dr. Everett Ferguson is a great scholar. I had him for one graduate religion class. He wrote the book *The Church of Christ* which is a tremendous resource from history and Scripture.

Fourth, Dr. Campbell wrote, "There really is only one Church of Christ. That's one of the cardinal claims of the ecumenical movement of the twentieth century, and the Churches of Christ were way out front in making us aware of that claim."

The New Testament teaches that the body is the church and the church is the body (Eph. 1:22-23 and Col. 1:18). It also teaches very clearly there is "one body" (Rom. 12:4-5; Col. 3:15; 1 Cor. 12:12, 13, 20; Eph. 4:4). If the body is the church and the church is the body, and there is only one body then there is only one church. Every figure that refers to the church teaches its oneness: one King--one kingdom (John 18:36); one husband--one bride (2 Cor. 11:2); one shepherd--one flock (John 10:11, 16; Eph. 2:12-22); one building--one foundation (1 Cor. 3:9, 11). According to Ephesians 4:5, there is also only "one faith" and "one baptism." It is not a matter of being high and mighty or arrogant or holier than thou, it is just the plain teaching of the New Testament that there is only "one church." Those faithful to the truth will teach and preach this doctrine.

Fifth, Dr. Campbell said, "Perhaps most importantly, the simplicity of the Churches of Christ allows them to focus on what is most important, namely, the Gospel of Jesus Christ. There was no congregational creed beyond the songs we sang, of course, but a member of the congregation got up before the offering and exhorted us to consider the sacrifice of Christ as we give ourselves."

Admittedly, the services in Churches of Christ are simple. Paul wrote, "But I fear, lest by any means, as the serpent beguiled Eve in his craftiness, your minds should be corrupted from the **simplicity** and the purity that is toward Christ" (2 Cor. 11:3). Services in the Churches of Christ do not seek to make an ostentatious show. We do not believe in wearing expensive robes. We do not seek to buy expensive crosses made out of gold or silver. We simply want to teach the truth of God's word. Several years ago, I took a Catholic lady to the church where I was attending. After the service, I asked her what she thought. She replied, "It was amazingly simple." Her comment made me think of 2 Corinthians 11:3.

Dr. Campbell concluded, "I came away with the sense that Churches of Christ folk really are the hobbits of the Christian world: not a lot of technological razzmatazz, not a lot of heavy emotion, not an elaborate or sophisticated liturgy, they just get the job done. There is a primitive simplicity to their communities that really stands out among other church bodies trying to be the church of Christ. We'd do well to learn from them and thank God for their witness." Notice his comment that "there is a primitive simplicity to their communities." Campbell observes us correctly. We want the focus of the worship service to be on the gospel message!

It is sad that some Churches of Christ are moving away from this "primitive simplicity." They are trying to appeal to the vanity of people by making the worship services an ostentatious show with praise teams and choirs and solos and piano playing. Church history testifies against solos and choirs and praise teams. John Chrysostom (347-407 A.D.) wrote, "It was the ancient custom as it still is with us for all to come together, all join in one song, all worldly distinctions here cease . . . and the whole congregation form one general chorus." McClintock and Strong state, "From the apostolic age singing was always a part of divine service, in which the whole body of the church joined together; and it was the decay of this practice that first brought the order of singers into the Church." *The Oxford Dictionary of the Christian Church* points out that at first singing was congregational, "but gradually the practice of having a body of trained singers was introduced." **The reflexive plural pronouns in Ephesians 5:18-19 and Colossians 3:16 strongly teach that God does not want praise teams and select choirs and solos in the worship service! What God requires is congregational singing.** Johnny Ramsey and Calvin Warpula debated on this subject. Calvin said that choirs and solos and praise teams are invigorating. Johnny pointed out that we do not go to the worship service to be entertained; we go to worship to obey God. Liberals say that solos and choirs and praise teams are entertaining and appeal to the unchurched. But, the question is do we violate God's plan when we appeal to the unchurched with a method that is anti-scriptural? Absolutely! God said a long time ago--"To obey is better than sacrifice" (1 Sam. 15:22).

Other Facts That Separate Us from Other Religious Groups

#1 We have no human creeds. The creed of the Church of Christ is the New Testament. We do not add to it or subtract from it (Deut. 4:2; Deut. 12:32; Prov. 30:5-6; Matt. 4:4; 1 Cor. 4:6; 1 Cor. 14:37; Gal. 3:15; 2 Tim. 3:16-17; Rev. 22:8-9). No uninspired men could make a creed or bind one on the Church. They could not then. They cannot now. The inspired Word is now an all-sufficient guide in all matters of religious faith, doctrine, and practice (2 Tim. 3:16-17).

#2 There is only "one baptism" (Eph. 4:5). This "one baptism" is water baptism "unto the remission of sins" (Acts 2:38). It is for those old enough to understand the gospel and obey it (Mark 16:15-16). Babies are in a safe condition and are not capable of obeying the gospel. Peter taught that baptism is in water (1 Pet. 3:20-21). Philip baptized the Eunuch in water (Acts 8:36-38). It takes "much water" to baptize (John 3:23). You can study the entire New Testament and you will never find a command "Be baptized in the Holy Spirit." Holy Spirit baptism was a promise and not a command. The promise was to a select few. In Joel 2:28-32 God prophesied that He would "pour out my Spirit upon all flesh." The words "all flesh" means all kinds of flesh which to a Jewish mind meant Jews and Gentiles. In Acts 2:33, the Jewish apostles received the promise of Joel. In Acts 10: 45, the

Holy Spirit was "poured out" on Cornelius's household (i.e. the Gentiles).

#3 There is no miraculous tongue speaking today. Some say that when you are baptized, you should speak in tongues--which proves your salvation. But, Paul taught that all Christians do not speak in tongues (1 Cor. 12:30). I would encourage the reader to read chapter 13 in my book ***Building Our Most Holy Faith*** which clearly demonstrates that all miracles have ceased today. No one is raising people from the dead today. No one is healing miraculously today. No one is speaking in tongues miraculously today.

#4 The doctrine of "Once Saved Always Saved" is false doctrine. It is possible to be in the church and still be lost. Paul said, "But the Spirit saith expressly, that in later times some shall fall away (depart KJV) from the faith, giving heed to seducing spirits and doctrines of demons" (1 Tim. 4:1). A person could not depart from the faith if he had never been in it. No king could abdicate a throne he had never occupied. No man could resign an office he had never held. So, when some say that if a person backslides into sin, he never was saved, his argument is false. This passage definitely declares that some who are saved will be lost. On the Day of Judgment the angels will take the kingdom (i.e. the Church) and shall "sever the wicked from among the righteous, and shall cast them into the furnace of fire" (Matt. 13:47-50). Therefore, not everyone in the kingdom (i.e. the Church) will be saved. Paul said in Galatians 5:4 that some of the Christians had fallen "out of" grace (Greek *ekpipto*). One cannot be saved without God's grace. You cannot fall from a place you have never been in. These Christians were within God's grace and had fallen out of it. This proves one is not "Once Saved Always Saved."

Conclusion

It is interesting that an outsider like Dr. Ted Campbell has observed our practices to be in accordance with the New Testament. We want to appeal to all members of the Church of Christ to **"Ask for the Old Paths"** and walk therein. God said if we do walk in the old paths, we would find rest for our souls (Jer. 6:16). We will be wise if we obey God and walk in the old paths. We will be foolish if we do not (Matt. 7:24-27).

For Thought or Discussion

1. What was Dr. Campbell's first observation?
2. Why do Churches of Christ have a "profound insight into Christian music and its place in worship?"
3. (True or False) The Old Testament never discusses the love of God.
4. (True or False) An instrument improves congregational singing.
5. Answer the argument—If you partake of the Lord's Supper every week, it will lose its meaning.
6. Why must we observe the Lord's Supper on Sunday and not Tuesday or some other day?
7. (True or False) Churches of Christ are being high and mighty and arrogant when they teach there is only one church.
8. (True or False) We are warned in Scripture about being corrupted from the simplicity that is in Christ.

9. What do church history and the New Testament teach about praise teams, choirs, and solos?
10. Do we violate God's plan when we appeal to the unchurched with a method that is anti-scriptural? Why?
11. (True or False) The key factor in worship is to do things that are invigorating.
12. What does 1 Samuel 15:22 teach?
13. Where in the New Testament is the command-- "Be baptized in the Holy Spirit?"
14. Where are the only two cases of Holy Spirit baptism found?
15. (True or False) Holy Spirit baptism was a promise and not a command.
16. (True or False) Miracles have ceased today.
17. What does Matthew 13:47-50 teach about being in the kingdom?
18. What does Galatians 5:4 teach about "Once Saved Always Saved?"

12

Is the Church of Christ a Cult?

Several years ago someone gave me a computer print-out of an article entitled "Is the Church of Christ a Cult?" No author's name was attached to the article. However, the Freedom Quest Ministries, PO Box 277, Calhan, Colorado, 80808 is given as the source for the article. In this chapter I want to present what they say compared to the truth of God's word! They state, "In this study guide we will endeavor to examine the claim of the Church of Christ to be God's sole representative on the earth today, and answer the question, Is the Church of Christ Denomination a Cult?"

#1 The **Church of Christ is not a denomination**. The Church of Christ that was started on the Day of Pentecost in Jerusalem was not part of anything. It was the whole. It was not divided up into different names, different organizations, different baptisms, different faiths, different types of worship, etc. When a person obeys the gospel, he is saved and the Lord adds him to the one true Church (Mark 16:16; Acts 2:38-47; Rom. 6:3-18). The Church of Christ has no earmarks of a denomination. We have no centralized headquarters, no president, no elected officers, no yearly meetings, etc. We have no creed book that we make members adhere to other then the Bible.

We do not even say that there is only one certain version
of the Bible that faithful Christians can use. (I must add
that many scholarly brethren in the Church of Christ
dislike certain versions. I am one of them. We will
continue to point out the mistranslation of certain verses-
-for example, the NIV translation of John 3:16.) We pay
no dues to a county, state, or national agency. We are
locally autonomous. Most people are shocked when they
hear this. The Baptists, Methodists, Presbyterians,
Lutherans, and others all have the basic earmarks of a
denomination. The Church of Christ seeks to return to
the New Testament as its only guide and authority in all
religious matters. In 1 Corinthians 1:13 Paul asked, "Is
Christ divided?" Of course the answer is no! Division is
sinful (Gal. 5:19-21).

#2 The article says, "Much of the organization is cultic."
The Church of Christ is not a cult! Webster defines a
cult as, "A quasi-religious group, often living in a colony,
with a charismatic leader who indoctrinates members
with unorthodox or extremist views, practices or beliefs."
We do not live in a colony. We have no charismatic
leader. Yes, we have some excellent preachers and
professors who teach the Bible. As long as they follow
the Bible, we will allow them to teach and preach (1 Cor.
11:1). When they leave the truth, we leave them. There
have been some leaders in the Church of Christ that have
gone into apostasy and they have been marked and
avoided (Rom. 16:17). It is true that some of our views
do not coincide with the views of the majority of the
religious world. But, Jesus said that many of His
followers would be surprised on the Day of Judgment
and not allowed into heaven (Matt. 7:21-23). Jesus also

said that only a "few" would enter heaven (Matt. 7:13-14). I quoted Matthew 7:13-14 to a fellow teacher and she responded, "I disagree." Jesus is the one who said it--not me. She was disagreeing with Jesus--not me. Faithful Christians need to expect opposition from the majority. Jesus said, "Woe unto you, when all men shall speak well of you!" (Luke 6:26). Therefore, the fact that we receive opposition and criticism helps to confirm our calling. If we never received criticism, we had better check our teaching. The article calls our beliefs "unorthodox." The word "unorthodox" means "not conforming to the usual beliefs or established doctrines, as in religion; specifically not conforming to the Christian faith as formulated in the early ecumenical creeds and confessions." We absolutely do not conform to the established creeds by men. Space does not permit the studying of all these man-made creeds. We do seek to conform to the doctrines of the Bible! Sometimes men get it wrong. This is why we must always go back to the Bible and follow the truth set forth therein. We must do what Jehovah wanted Judah to do, **"Ask for the old paths, where is the good way; and walk therein, and ye shall find rest for your souls"** (Jer. 6:16). When people call me unorthodox, I think yes I reject man-made creeds and man-made doctrines, but I accept the Christian faith as revealed in the New Testament. People can call us a cult, but we seek to follow God's word in all religious matters. If others see us as people that do not go along with the established beliefs and practices of the majority, they are correct. But, remember many will be surprised on the Day of Judgment and will not enter heaven, and only a "few" will enter therein! I would like to present a true story. Around 1992, I was grading papers with about 40 teachers in a math contest. The majority thought the answer key was wrong on one problem. I agreed with the majority. There was one teacher who was adamant and said the answer key was right. We all respected this particular teacher's scholarship and education. If you accepted the majority, he lost 40 to 1. He was extremely adamant he was right. So, we decided to accept the answer key and his view. At that time I still thought he was wrong. When I got home and researched the problem, I discovered he was right! This example teaches that sometimes the minority is right and the majority is wrong. This example can also be applied to interpreting the Bible. Please remember the majority on the Day of Judgment will be wrong and will lose their eternal souls. So, I am not seeking to be with the majority who accept established doctrines that are wrong according to the Bible. I want to be in the minority with the "few" who are going to heaven (Matt. 7:13-14).

#3 The Church of Christ did not start in 1906 or the mid 1800s. The article stated, "In 1906 the Church of Christ Denomination broke away from the Christian church which was established in the mid 1800s by Alexander Campbell during the so-called Restoration Movement." They also said, "Alexander Campbell initiated the Restoration Movement in the mid 1800s." Whoever wrote this is just plain ignorant. He needs to read Bill Humble's book *"The Story of the Restoration"* and books by Adrian Doran and Earl West and others. Alexander Campbell did not start the Church of Christ in America. To make this claim is ignorance!

#4 The article denies "the belief that you are born again and receive your salvation at the moment of water baptism." The writer(s) are just ignorant of the truth concerning Mark 16:16 and John 3:5 and Acts 2:38 and Acts 22:16 and 1 Peter 3:21. Please study chapters 9 and 10 and 13 in my book *Searching for Biblical Truth* where this article's false teaching is answered with the truth of Scripture and New Testament Greek grammar!

#5 The article says, "We know for a fact that the thief died under the New Covenant." Jesus told the penitent thief, "Today shalt thou be with me in Paradise." Yes, this was before Jesus died. This was when the Old Covenant was still in effect. The article states, "So if the New Covenant was ushered in at the death of our Lord and Savior, Jesus Christ, then anyone who died from that point on, died under the New Covenant. And that would include the thief on the cross." Yes, the thief died after Jesus. But, the New Covenant did not go into effect until the Day of Pentecost. The command of Acts 2:38, "Repent ye, and be baptized every one of you in the name of Jesus Christ unto the remission of your sins" did not apply to the thief because he died before that command went into effect. Jesus saved others besides the thief on the cross before he died.

#6 The writer(s) miss Colossians 2:11-12 . Here Paul says, "In whom ye were also circumcised with a circumcision not made with hands, in the putting off of the body of the flesh, in the circumcision of Christ; having been buried with him in baptism, wherein ye were also raised with him through faith in the working of God, who raised him from the dead." The circumcision Paul is discussing here is not a physical one--in the putting off of

the body of the flesh. Paul is discussing a spiritual one--
the circumcision not made with hands. This spiritual
circumcision occurs when one is "buried with him in
baptism." It is at the point of baptism that we are
baptized into His death and come into contact with His
saving blood!

#7 The writer(s) claim that baptism is just symbolic.
What was the walking around the city of Jericho a total
of 13 times? Was it just symbolic or a command to
obey? What was the Pool of Siloam to the blind man?
Was it just symbolic or a command to obey? We, those
in the Churches of Christ, believe the water in baptism
saves no one. Just like the water in the Pool of Siloam
did not heal the blind man. But, the water of the Pool of
Siloam became the absolute necessary channel of
obedience that brought about his sight. Baptism is much
more than just symbolic!

#8 The writer(s) claim that Acts 16:31 teaches that all
one has to do to be saved is "Believe in the Lord Jesus."
In chapter 12 of my book *Searching for Biblical Truth*, I
have a whole chapter devoted to a study of Acts 16:31. I
would encourage the reader to read and study this
chapter. It shows how many twist, distort, pervert, and
wrest Scripture from its correct meaning (2 Pet. 3:15-17).

#9 The writer(s) use the case of Cornelius. They state,
"Clearly we have in this example, a case where a person
was obviously saved before he was water baptized."
Again, I deal with this case in chapter 9 of my book
Searching for Biblical Truth. The article states, "The
only way around this scenario is to deny that a person is
filled with the Holy Spirit (evidenced by speaking in

tongues and glorifying God) is actually saved. And believe it or not, that is exactly what the CHOCD says! It never ceases to amaze me what some people are willing to swallow in order to protect what they feel is biblical, even if it denies the very Bible they seek to uphold." The Holy Spirit baptism on the lost Cornelius was a fulfillment of prophecy. Joel 2 predicted that the Holy Spirit would be poured out on "all flesh." "All flesh" means Jews and Gentiles. The Jews would be those in a covenant relationship with God. These were the apostles--John 15:3; Acts 1:26-2:4. The Gentiles would be those not in a covenant relationship with God. If not in a covenant relationship, they would be lost. True? In Acts 10:45 the Holy Spirit was "poured out" on the lost Cornelius thus fulfilling Scripture. If God can talk through a donkey, why can't He talk through unsaved people? The purpose of the Holy Spirit baptism on Cornelius was to convince Peter that Gentiles were now acceptable candidates to come into the kingdom/church (Acts 10:47-48). Notice in Acts 10:48 that baptism is a command. It is not optional. We cannot take the difficult passages and explain away the easy ones. One rule of hermeneutics is always to interpret the difficult passages in light of the clear, simple, and plain verses!

#10 The article says, "It is really the Apostle Paul that puts the icing on the cake on the issue of baptism, by stating in 1 Corinthians 1:17, 'Christ did **not** send me to baptize, **but** to preach the gospel.' Now if baptism is the point of salvation, this statement would be utterly blasphemous." Here the writer(s) really show their ignorance. 1 Corinthians 1:17 is a relative negation, a

"not-but" passage. When you have a **"not-but"** passage, be very careful how you interpret it! Do not take the not phrase as an absolute. This is what many do and they make a big mistake! Why does God use relative negations? For emphasis! It contrasts in a strong way the spiritual truth God wants us to learn. After the word **"not"** you can insert the word only or merely or just to obtain the correct meaning. There is an ellipsis in a "not-but" passage. After the word **"but,"** you can insert the words "most importantly." (Research John 12:44 and John 6:27 and chapter 9 in my book *Searching for Biblical Truth*.) The point of 1 Corinthians 1:10-17 is that anyone can do the baptizing. The most important thing is to preach the gospel. Paul did baptize people. Did Paul have a different gospel to preach than the other apostles? Of course not! The other apostles were sent to baptize (Matt. 28:18-20; Mark 16:15-16). Did Paul sin when he did baptize? Of course not! Are we to believe that the original twelve apostles were sent to baptize but Paul was not? No! Paul was using the "not-but" to emphasize the point that the first step is to preach the gospel. He was also making the point that who does the baptizing is not the important thing.

#11 The writer(s) set forth the position that we believe that baptism is a work in which we earn our salvation. They say, "Salvation is a gift that no one can earn." We agree totally with the writers that salvation cannot be earned! We do not believe that baptism earns our salvation. Paul wrote, "We are saved by grace (God's unmerited favor) through faith (a steadfast trust conjoined with obedience)" (Eph. 2:8). It is our obedient faith that brings about God's favor and our salvation.

James 2:26 states, "Faith apart from works is dead." Our faithful obedience does not mean we earned it. Luke 17:10 clearly teaches our faithful obedience cannot earn our salvation! Hebrews 11:30 states, "By faith the walls of Jericho fell down." What caused the walls of Jericho to fall down? An obedient faith! Faith is our part in the salvation process. But, the faith that saves is the faith that obeys. Baptism is an act of faith (Col. 2:12) that brings about salvation. Baptism does not mean we have earned salvation. Baptism is just the point or moment of our faith/obedience that brings about our salvation (Mark 16:16; Rom. 6:17-18).

#12 The writer(s) laugh at our staunch arguments against musical instruments in worship. They state, "The Bible very clearly does give us permission to have musical instruments in our worship to God." Their main argument is over the Old Testament word "psalm." They cite *Strong's Exhaustive Concordance of the Bible* which defines "psalm" as "a set piece of music, i.e. a sacred ode (accompanied with the voice, harp, or other instrument)." We do not disagree with *Strong's Concordance*. But, very simply the point is that was under the Old Covenant. We agree that God allowed musical instruments under the Old Covenant. But, God also allowed polygamy, animal sacrifice, incense, the Levitical priesthood, etc. But, does He allow those things now? Absolutely not! They want to call musical instruments in worship as "non-essential issues." We vehemently disagree with this position. Read the chapter on Worship in this book.

#13 The writer(s) accuse us of being legalistic. I have to agree with them to a point. Yes, some brethren in the Church of Christ are legalists. Legalism is binding where God has loosed. Liberalism is loosing where God has bound. Both are wrong. We have some ignorant brethren who want to bind the KJV on all Christians. These brethren state that all other versions are false, spurious, and not God's word. This is just ignorance gone to seed. Some brethren say that only one cup must be used in the Lord's Supper. Sadly, I could go on and on with these aberrations in the Church of Christ. Even though problems exist in the Churches of Christ, this does not change the truth. Not all brethren are legalistic.

#14 The authors of the article give an example of adultery, divorce, and then marriage. They really did not do their homework on this item. We do believe that adultery gives one the right to remarry. The example of the Church of Christ preacher they give is a complete aberration from the norm. Yes, sadly, the Church that Jesus died for gets a black eye in this case. We deny that we are legalists. We demand an obedience of faith, but that is Scriptural (Rom. 1:5; 16:26)! If they want to call us legalists because we demand an obedience of faith, so be it! Jesus said, "Woe unto you, when all men speak well of you" (Luke 6:26).

#15 The writer(s) do not understand the ministry of the Holy Spirit. They claim, "The promise of receiving the baptism of the Holy Spirit was for every believer." Absolutely not! The promise of being baptized in the Holy Spirit in Acts 1:5-8 was for the apostles only. Read the text carefully. Notice Acts 1:26-2:4. The antecedent of the word "they' in Acts 2:1 is the word "apostles" in

Acts 1:26. The promise of "remission of sins" and "the gift of the Holy Spirit" was for every believer (Acts 2:38-39). "The gift of the Holy Spirit" does not enable Christians to work miracles. Many in the Church of Christ believe "the gift of the Holy Spirit" is the personal indwelling in the Christian by the Holy Spirit that serves as a promise (Greek *arrabon*) that one day the Lord will return and take us to heaven. The Greek word *arrabon* was used of earnest money in buying a house and also as an engagement ring. "The gift of the Holy Spirit" also becomes a motive to abstain from sin (1 Cor. 6:12-20). I would encourage the reader to read chapter 13 in my book *Building Our Most Holy Faith.*

#16 The article says, "So are they a cult? No. Are they as close as you can get to the edge of that perilous pit without falling in? Based on the Word of God, I would say an emphatic 'Yes.'" At least they say we are not a cult.

#17 The writers wanted to defend the translation of the Greek preposition *eis* in Acts 2:38 as "because of." A. Oepke, in his lengthy article in *Kittel's Theological Dictionary of the New Testament*, says the word *eis* in Acts 2:38 denotes "the direction of an action to a specific end." That is, it conveys purpose or design toward an unreached goal, and not cause of a past result (Vol. II, p.429). *Arndt and Gingrich Greek Lexicon* define *eis* in Acts 2:38 "so that sins might be forgiven" (second ed., p. 229). The Greek of Acts 2:38 is the same as the Greek of Matthew 26:28. Did Jesus go to the cross because the sins of man had already been remitted or did He go to the cross to remit the sins of man? Their scholarship is woefully lacking! Research chapter 9 in my book *Searching for Biblical Truth*.

Conclusion

There is always a benefit of being academically challenged and reading material you do not agree with. It makes you study harder. Reading this article has helped me do just that. It also has allowed me to see the fallacies of these writers. My second doctor's degree was from Trinity Theological Seminary in Newburg, Indiana. This seminary is heavily Calvinistic. However, that fact made me study much harder and I came to the conclusion that Calvinism is wrong.

For Thought or Discussion

1. Prove the Church of Christ is not a denomination.
2. Define the words "cult" and "unorthodox."
3. (True or False) Faithful Christians need to expect opposition from the majority.
4. (True or False) Christians need to conform to the established man-made creeds so they can be "orthodox." Why?
5. What do Matthew 7:13-14 and Matthew 7:21-23 teach?
6. (True or False) Alexander Campbell started the Church of Christ in America.
7. Why could the thief on the cross not obey Acts 2:38?
8. (True or False) The Church of Christ believes that the water saves one.
9. Discuss the blind man and the Pool of Siloam.
10. Discuss the baptism of the Holy Spirit and Cornelius.

11. Explain a relative negation using John 6:27 and 1 Cor. 1:17.

12. (True or False) In a relative negation or "not-but" passage, one needs to take the not phrase as an absolute!

13. (True or False) Our faithful obedience means we are earning our salvation.

14. What does Luke 17:10 teach?

15. (True or False) Musical instruments in worship is a "non-essential issue."

16. (True or False) Some brethren in the Church of Christ are legalistic.

17. What is the difference between legalism and liberalism?

18. What did Jesus say in Luke 6:26? What is the significance?

19. (True or False) The promise of receiving the baptism of the Holy Spirit was for every believer. Prove.

20. (True or False) Speaking in tongues is proof that a Christian is saved. Scripture?

21. (True or False) Jesus gave all the truth on marriage and divorce when He was on the earth? (1 Cor. 7:10-15)

About the Author

Dr. John Hobbs was born and reared in Fort Worth, Texas. His parents are Carlton and Peggy Hobbs. His uncle, A. G. Hobbs Jr. was a gospel preacher who wrote the "Hobbs Series of Gospel Tracts." These can now be purchased from John Hobbs. His aunt, Lottie Beth Hobbs, has written several ladies' books for classroom studies. Both A. G. and Lottie were listed by *The Gospel Advocate* in the 100 most influential Christians in the 20th century. In 1973, John married Mary Etta Palmer, daughter of Roy and Jaxie Palmer, who were missionaries to Germany and Africa. John and Mary Etta have four sons: Carlton Allen, William Palmer, Austin Bennett, and Mark Alexander.

Dr. John Hobbs has earned the following degrees: BSE, MA, MDivinity from Abilene Christian University; ME from North Texas State University; MS from Amber University; MA from Dallas Baptist University; the Doctor of Ministry in Church Growth from Harding Graduate School of Religion in Memphis, Tennessee; and the Doctor of Ministry in Theology from Trinity Theological Seminary in Newburgh, Indiana. He has also graduated from the Sunset School of Preaching Extension Department in Lubbock, Texas and the Southern Baptist Convention Seminary Extension Department in Nashville, Tennessee. Including graduate audit courses John has 604 college hours in biblically related subjects. Presently, he is still taking Bible courses.

John has written eleven other books: *The Word Was God*; *Searching for Biblical Truth*; *Building Our Most Holy Faith*; *Seeking Spiritual Strength*; *The Compelling Power of the Cross*; *Never, Never, Never Give Up!*; *The Ten Commandments*; *Greek Notes over 1,2,3 John*; *Advanced Bible Study*; *The Sermon on the Mount*; and *Number Sense Makes Cents*. These last five books listed are "loose-leaf" books. All of these books can be ordered from Dr. John Hobbs at 1106 Destiny Court, Wylie, Texas, 75098.

John preached his first sermon at the age of fourteen. He has been preaching for over 50 years. All his local works have been in Texas. He has preached for the Church of Christ in Hamby (1970-1973); Loving (1974-1979); Lakeview in Grand Prairie (1979-1982); Cold Springs in Lancaster (1982-1996); Lawn (1996-1998); Hillcrest in Coleman (1998-2002); Ninth and Main in San Angelo (2002-2005); Cottonwood in Wylie (2005-2007); and Sachse (2008 to present). Lakeview grew from 89 to 185 with 53 baptisms and a record high of 277. Cold Springs grew from 48 to 156 with 88 baptisms and a record high of 225. Lawn grew from 41 to 86 with 6 baptisms and a record high of 122. Ninth and Main grew from 65 to 100 with 22 baptisms and a record high of 137. Cottonwood grew from 56 to 114 with 15 baptisms and a record high of 188. Presently, the Sachse congregation is growing also.

The author encourages the reader to write him with comments about the book.

41759293R00098

Made in the USA
Charleston, SC
10 May 2015